Kindest Regards—Have a
purrfect day.
        Idabelle
          &
          Blackie

A Cat of Many Tales

...from the Journals of "Ice" Berg

... a true sophistiCat

as recorded and illustrated by
Idabelle I. Berg

A Cat
of Many Tales

...from the Journals of "Ice" Berg

by Idabelle L. Berg

ISBN 0-9646803-8-6
First Edition, First Printing

PLANT*Speak Publications
34100 Center Ridge Road, N. Ridgeville, OH 44039
Phone/fax 440-327-5059 e-mail plantspeak@aol.com

Dedication

In memory of my mother, Mary Peabody, to whom I am grateful for encouraging my interest in art and for passing on to me a share of her artistic abilities.

Idabelle L. Berg

A Special Thank-You

To Ma's sister, Vivian -- who is also my aunt -- for her support and encouragement, and to Ma's husband, Charles -- also my Pa -- for his patience and understanding. Both have been an inspiration to Ma and me for this mutual endeavor.

***

I hope you will enjoy reading the story of my life, thus far. If you are concerned about the language and terminology used, and think it is beyond the intelligence of a cat, you are almost right. For, without the help of Ma, I would not have been able to write this story and I will always be *eat-ernally* grateful to her.

Blackie "Ice" Berg

Contents

List of Illustrations

Mom-Mew

Idabelle Berg's Art

During her childhood, Idabelle Berg became interested in drawing, and was encouraged by her mother, who was herself a fine pen and ink illustrator. Idabelle started to do sketches, using charcoal and pencil, in grade school. During her early years, she managed to take a few art lessons from local artists as she moved on to do pen and ink renderings and later completed a few paintings using oils. Her switch to acrylics and watercolors came gradually, and she says that water colors are now her favorite medium. Basically self-taught, in recent years she has enjoyed watching and taking notes from artists as they demonstrated their work on television. Her paintings have won several local and State Grange Blue Ribbons and very recently a painting titled, "Barnyard Gossip," was honored with an award in a Grange artists' national competition.

We like the home-spun quality, the basic simplicity and unassuming nature of her paintings and find touches of inspiration, if not genius, in her attention to emotive detail. Although her watercolors seem primitive in aspect, Berg paints abandonment, anger, guilt, surprise, fear, curiosity, concern, longing, and joy in the eyes of her subjects, and she sees tiny creatures, such as a cricket or a worm, through the magnifying eyes of her beloved cat.

For example, look closely at her rendition of Ice as he laughs at cat cartoons. We almost do not notice the large marble and its reflection in the forefront of the painting. We chuckle as we look upon the heaped-over "Ice" as he tries to figure out how the "walking feather" moves; and, we feel the charge between "Ice" and the giant tomato worm as they eyeball each other -- while the butterflies, the birds and the snake go obliviously on their ways through the otherwise quiet meadow.

Above all, Idabelle manages to transfer to her watercolors the love she has for nature and the family farm which occupies the heart of her world. That she does all this from a small drawing board located in a spare bedroom on the second floor of her Henrietta farm home seems miraculous to us. For these obvious reasons, and as a reflection of her indomitable spirit, we are proud to share her art and her cat stories with you .

P*S

Foreword

Like so many pathetic, similar cases, Mom-Mew, apparently unwanted, had been dropped off, by a very uncaring, irresponsible person or persons, at the door of Old Man and Old Woman. This was a very inhumane act toward both Mom-Mew and the old couple, for they were very feeble and Mow-Mew, especially in her condition, would prove to be a burden to them.

Seeing she was pregnant, Old Man and Old Woman decided to take Mom-Mew in until she had her kittens. Old Man and Old Woman had lived a long and rewarding life and they must have considered all life very precious, for they were willing to take on the responsibility of seeing to it that Mom-Mew would be given every chance to have a healthy litter.

Soon, Mom-Mew, really just an ordinary house cat, but noted as one of the world's most protective and caring mothers, had her kittens. And, what adorable little balls of fluff they were!

Old Man and Old Woman were old in age and in spirit, so they were able to care for Mom-Mew and her kittens for only one year. It was just long enough to enable them to appreciate the wonder of new life again, and to allow the kittens to develop to the point at which they could physically fend for themselves.

Of all truths on this great earth blue,
I have a great mom and so do you!
No matter where we go or how we do,
Our mothers' love is always true.

1

First Year

$\mathcal{M}$om, that is Mom-Mew, was proud of her three kittens, two handsome boys and one pretty girl. There was brother Bo, sister Fluff, and me...Blackie. We were balls of fluff and, of course, always as good as we could be. Our days were filled with fun and frolic. There was no substitute for Mom-Mew. She was our guarantee of safety and happiness for all our todays and all our tomorrows.

Mom-Mew was beautiful. She looked very distinguished in her silver gray coat of fur. Brother Bo was a tiger cat, with very distinct ring markings, especially on his tail, which made him look a little bit like a raccoon. Sister Fluff was a soft cream-color with thick long fur. I was black as night, except for a very small splash of white on my chest. That's why my given name is Blackie.

We were a happy feline family. We were very typical kittens; carefree, curious and mischievous. Brother Bo, sister Fluff and I spent most of our first year in a very modest home. It was there that we grew strong and developed our cat skills under the not-too-sharp eyes of Old Man and Old Woman.

We could spend many happy moments batting a clothespin across the linoleum floor in the kitchen, sending it to the far corner of the room. Old Woman hung Old Man's underwear on a short line close to the pot-bellied stove and usually failed to pick up items, such as clothespins and the like, when dropped. Whether this was from poor memory or a lack of exertion on her part, we really weren't interested in knowing, as long as it provided us with unending entertainment.

Old Woman was getting up in years and her house-keeping was less than desired, but she always kept our bed, food dishes and litter pan clean, which really was not an easy task, with the four of us. One day, with our welfare in mind, she brought in a used, but now discarded bell, and added it to our growing assortment of playthings. The bell at one time may have been worn around the neck of a farm animal, perhaps a sheep, goat or cow, to keep track of the animal's whereabouts. The bell would tinkle, or clang, the intensity of the sound, depending on how hard it was hit. We liked to send it flying across the smooth floor, the louder the sound the more exciting to us. It provided us with many happy hours of fun, notwithstanding the noise that Old Man and Old Woman had to endure.

Our bed was a large cardboard box, lined with dis-carded wool underwear, no doubt previously worn by Old Man. The soft wool made our bed comfortably warm and cozy, especially when all of us chose to lie in it at one time. Our box was on one side of the pot-bellied stove and another large box, filled with firewood, was on the other.

We were thankful for the extra heat from the stove, seeing how cold it was outside that first winter.

As we grew older, although our claws were still too immature, we tried to imitate Mom-Mew as she sharpened her's on the wood in the wood box. Some of the wood, when placed in the stove by Old Man or Old Woman, gave off a pungent aroma, almost as tantalizing as catnip.

Mealtime was always pleasurable, despite the fact that I was usually late and would have to take the place least comfortable, which was always near the back. Mom-Mew would accommodate me by holding her leg up until I was in position to nurse, and then gently rest it back over me. This was not all bad for it gave me an extra sense of security. Occasionally, I'd fall asleep while nursing and come up a little short on my meal, when Mom-Mew signaled that dinner was over by disengaging herself from us and would move off, her action proclaiming it was time for her to be alone for a while.

We never tired of playing with the window shade tassel. Sometimes we tugged so hard the shade would fly to the top of the window, scaring Old Woman, to our delight, if she were nearby. She would retort with a few harsh words, directed at us, as she pulled the shade back down, and we scattered to a safe haven. But we couldn't resist the temptation, and would only repeat our fun by having a go at it another day.

Old Man seemed to care less about our antics as he sat in his favorite chair, chewing something that made one of his cheeks puff way out like a big rolling bubble. Every now and then, he would leave his chair, to go over to a rather elegant cuspidor, which was really one of Old Woman's pretty jardinieres. Incidentally, that jardiniere was sitting dangerously close to our bed. Old Man would stop over the jardiniere and, sometimes making a loud sound, "Spit-too-eee!", shoot a golden stream of liquid into it.

3

Settling back in his chair, he would wipe his mouth adeptly with the back of his hand, to catch some of the golden liquid that had dribbled down his chin. I always thought that Old Man was very foolish in his habit of doing this, for it seemed to do him no earthly good at all. It seemed especially strange, for none of us had ever seen him pull up any grass to chew on, like we all soon learned to do. I later learned that Old Man was chewing tobacco, a very unhealthy enterprise which, in all likelihood, led him to an early demise. However, I liked to watch him, as he performed this unsanitary, and unhealthy, ritual. I was always amazed at how content he looked when he resumed his chewing with more normal looking cheeks. As I now consider his awful habit, it seems to me that Old Man was not so far removed from certain lower animal species, like cows. The difference was obvious, however. Old Man could have broken his habit by himself, whereas most animals have no control over their natural inclinations, and most animal habits, like the cows' chewing their cuds, have positive and practical benefits to the animal. Old Man's chewing activity would be repeated for hours, much to Old Woman's disgust and our continuing fear that he would miss the jardiniere and make an unwanted deposit of the gold-colored fluid in our bed!

One day, in the absence of Old Man, as Old Woman placed a piece of wood in the stove, she slipped on some of the golden fluid on the floor, where Old Man had missed the jardiniere. Old Woman was lucky. We were thankful that she was able to catch herself before falling, by grabbing hold of a nearby table. We were not around later, but I'm sure Old Woman had some rather choice words of admonishment for Old Man, when he returned. One thing I've learned over my lifetime, one's own bad habits have a very nasty way of harming others. I've often wondered how Old Man could be so careless regarding his unsanitary habit.

All in all, we were happy and healthy kittens. As days passed we grew bigger and stronger. We were also becoming more mature. Consequently, we were less apt to get into trouble. We soon outgrew our habit of pulling on the window shade tassel and startling poor Old Woman. Of course, Old Woman was pretty smart, too. She had learned some time ago to simply leave the shade rolled up at the top of the window, far out of our reach.

When we were finally weaned from our daily nursing, Old Woman added extra food and water dishes for the four of us. She was very meticulous about keeping our dishes clean and our bed free of this and that, which, now that we were more active, always seemed to accumulate.

Spring arrived and we were approaching our first birthdays. Becoming more responsible for ourselves, we were allowed to explore the great outdoors for longer periods of time. As Old Man and Old Woman did not move very fast anymore, it was easy to sneak out the door as they went in and out doing their few daily chores. We didn't venture too far away, as the world outside, to us, was vast, mysterious, and seemingly dangerous. We had a fear of getting locked outside and possibly having to deal with some of those creatures who made strange noises during the night. We were still at the age to value our security. We certainly weren't old enough to be real brave. We were content in those days just to chase a butterfly, to nibble on a blade of grass, to tumble and toss around with each other, or just to bask in the warm sunshine.

Then, one morning, we awoke to find Mom-Mew gone! Although we were already quite independent and really did not need her close attention and care any longer, we sorely missed her presence. No longer would we be able to tease our Mom-Mew by pulling on her tail, or simply rub up against her side to show our love for her. Her disappearance was a mystery to us; but, as the days and weeks passed, we gradually stopped worrying about her. Slowly, as the three of us, brother Bo, sister Fluff, and I, relied more and more on each other, we came to truly appreciate each other's company.

Bo, Blackie, Fluff

Though times be good or times be rough
Treat all others like a sister, like a brother
Always give of your love more than enough
To share abundantly with one another.

2

Loss of Litter Mates

*T*hat morning I awoke with a sense of foreboding. Brother Bo and sister Fluff had left the bed unusually early. Most mornings we awoke together. As we stretched out the kinks from our sound slumber, we would plan the days' schedule of activities and explorations. I resolved immediately to go looking for them. Perhaps they had already run off to awaken Old Man and Old Woman, which we quite often did together. A hurt feeling passed through me, to think that they had not thought to include me this morning. I scampered to the bedroom, only to find no-one about. How strange! And my feeling of foreboding intensified. Could it be that Bo and Fluff had gone somewhere with Old Man and Old Woman? Why had they left me all alone?

There was nothing for me to do but wait for them to return. I busied myself by eating some breakfast. It was not at all any fun eating alone, and, besides, the events so far this morning had dampened my usually good appetite. So, I ate very little. I crept back to our familiar bed, hoping to draw comfort from their imagined presence. I tried to think where and why they all had gone, and decided to nap, sure that they'd all be there when I would awaken again. No sooner had I dozed off, when I heard the familiar sound of the car pull into the drive. Glory-be, they had come home! I ran to the window to peer out. Old Man and Old Woman were coming up the walk alone! Perhaps Bo and Fluff had run ahead and were already at the door waiting to be let in. I couldn't wait for the door to open, but when it did, there was no Bo or Fluff! My heart sank. I thought certainly Old Woman must have heard my inner cry of disappointment, but when she glanced at me, she looked hurriedly away, seemingly unconcerned.

All that day, I remember, I kept watching for Fluff and Bo. In fact, I kept watching for many days. But no Bo and no Fluff; I had lost my brother and my sister, my litter mates, my world. Weeks passed, and I gradually gave up hope that I would ever see them again.

I began to spend more and more time outdoors, gradually immersing myself in the wonders of nature. There was always something interesting to do. If I wasn't in the mood for rough-housing around, I could always find a nice peaceful spot to lay, especially on a sunny day, where I could soak up the warmth of the sun's rays. Catching field mice was always a challenging sport. It was time consuming and required great patience. Sometimes I would sit for hours, not moving a muscle, to keep from giving my presence away and scaring off my quarry. I got to be very good at catching a nice fat mouse. It seemed to be so natural for me to hunt, and I was too young to give it a second thought. Most of the time I would simply cart the mouse off to the back door and offer it to Old Woman.

But Old Woman never appreciated my gift, and, upon finding it when she went outside, always lifted it with a paper towel and flung it far out in the back, away from the house, where it must have made a good meal for Mr. Owl or Mr. Hawk, for seldom did I see it lay long enough to be covered by swarms of blowflies.

As I look back on that day, I realize that the image of blowflies is harsh and lacking in sensitivity, but the image is a truth of nature, and nature's creatures seem sometimes to be involved in insensitive cruelties toward one another. This is an observation not normally made by any cat, and certainly not by a kitten! In fact, such observations are often made by humans, who are very sensitive to any mistreatment of animals, especially any mistreatment of animals by other humans. I have tried to understand such things and, as you will see, have learned much from humans as a result of my having been domesticated. It is my hope that, having learned some civility, some of it will rub off on those humans less sensitive than others to the plight of animals. Goodness sakes! I have become somewhat philosophical in my maturity! In any event, I always wondered why Old Woman never seemed to appreciate my mouse-giving generosity, goodness knows I kept trying to please her!

Every kitten needs a home
Where they are loved so much
They never have to roam
To purr alone or lose their mother's touch.

3

Abandoned

*I*t was wake-up time. I could hear Old Woman moving about a little faster and doing more chores than normal that morning. For one thing, she had placed an extra measure of fish in my food dish. It was so delectable. I thought I was still dreaming. Come to think of it, I thought I had smelled that aroma the night before, as Old Woman was preparing supper. Evidently she had some fish left over, or maybe she had purposely saved a piece for my special breakfast that day. I remember, as I savored every delicious morsel of that fish, Old Woman continued to busy herself about the room. Meanwhile, I noticed Old Man had left the house.

A feeling of impending disaster crept into my being. It was the same feeling I had had when Bo and Fluff disappeared. It was not long before I heard Old Man bringing the car up to the house. The motor was left running. In a few moments he entered the house. Hardly before I knew what was happening, Old Woman had gathered me up in her arms, to my mind holding me much more securely than seemed necessary. Out we all went to the car. Old Man held the door open as Old Women entered, holding me securely in her lap. You can under-stand me when I admit from that day on I distrusted cars. In fact, from that day on, every car became to me a *mechanical monster.*

Of course, I wondered where we were all going so early in the morning. The birds had not even begun to chirp yet. I didn't know it then, but I was the only one going somewhere to stay! The softness of Old Woman's lap felt comforting, and the taste of that great breakfast still lingered on my lips. I could not imagine our destination and, certainly, I had no reason to think any destination that day would be unhappy for me. I remember thinking that maybe they were taking me to see Bo and Fluff, and the pleasant thought of seeing them again made a feeling of warmth flow through my body.

After a short drive, Old Man steered the mechanical monster into a driveway. Old Man, being very gallant, and belying his somewhat unkempt appearance, came around to our side of the car and opened the door for us. Old Woman kept a tight grip on me as she got out of the car. She walked a short distance, then abruptly bent down, setting me on the ground in the gravel. The gravel seemed somewhat familiar to me, although it was coarser than what I was used to in my litter box. Strange how I remember it was much the same color as my litter box gravel and it smelled as clean. Old Man joined us. He carried a box of my cat food. He poured what was left of it out on the ground in a pile beside me. I remember looking up at them both. After a short pause, they turned away. I heard Old Woman sigh as they walked back to the car. Then I heard the deafening roar of their mechanical monster as they headed back down the road, without me. Had they really abandoned me? It takes time for cruel truth to sink deeply.

There I sat, in utter despair. I glanced at the heap of dry cat food beside me. I had always relished eating that food. Almost automatically, I began to eat. But I thought, as I ate then, that I would never eat that kind of cat food again. In fact, I resolved to never eat again. I was so saddened by what Old Man and Old Woman had done to me. No, saddened is not the right word. I was so distraught that I came very near to losing the fine fish breakfast I had eaten that morning. I don't like to admit this, but I could not hold back the moisture that filled my eyes as I resigned myself to a time of fitful waiting. Old Man and Old Woman would have to come back for me, I was sure. Though I had resolved to eat no more, I did not stray from the pile of food, deciding to hunch down next to it and try to nap. But, I seemed suspended in a state between, half wide awake and half napping.

Finally, the sun began to dawn, it seemed to shine upon a vast world of emptiness. I looked all around me, searching for something familiar, but there was nothing. The awful truth then dawned on me: Truly, I *had* been abandoned! I stayed crouched beside that little pile of food for what seemed like an eternity. My whole being was frozen in fear as I wondered what was to become of me. I was conscious of the birds singing their wake up songs. That sound seemed to lift my spirits somewhat. But moments later, my spirits again sank as I heard the plaintive whistle of a far off train. A church bell chimed, actually seemed to peal, off in the distance. Occasionally a mechanical monster would roar by. Once, one of them slowed and turned into the parking lot. I remember thinking that Old Man and Old Woman had finally come back for me. My spirits soared; oh, happy day; oh, if it were only true; I would love those poor old people forever! I even promised to suppress my instinctive desire to bring mice to the back door for Old Woman, since it had seemed to displease her so. Alas, the car made a complete circle in the parking lot, and didn't stop at all. It was only someone turning around to go back down the road.

My despair grew deeper as the morning hours went by slowly. Reflecting back, considering my present dilemma, I remember wondering if Old Man and Old Woman had had something to do with the mysterious disappearance of my mother. Had they done the same with Mom-Mew, *and* with Bo and Fluff? I knew that they were not capable of keeping us. They were feeble, and we must have been a burden to them. But, I wondered: Had they done all they could to try to find us another home?

The sun gradually moved higher in the deep blue sky. Normally, I would have been getting hungry by then. But, I remember how my stomach churned when I looked at the pile of food beside me. I looked away. Shortly thereafter, a mechanical monster came to a stop in the parking lot. My hopes rose a little. Another monster followed, and then another and another. I remember thinking that it was getting much too dangerous to stay there, out in the open. I was stiff from crouching in one position for so long a time, but I managed to run toward the shelter of a nearby building. I hid under a bush, close to the steps. I knew if I kept very quiet, I could stay concealed and safe.

Many people were going up the steps into the white-spired building. Shortly, I was startled by the loud pealing of a bell. Though loud and, to my ear, extremely piercing, the sound reminded me somehow of the bell that Bo, Fluff, and I had so many happy hours playing with when we were kittens. On the other hand, I had heard that bells sometimes toll for a funeral. At first I thought that, if it was a funeral, it might as well be mine. But then, I surprised myself with my own spirit of independence, for I recall muttering, "By gosh, no way am I going to attend my own funeral!"

Soon, I could hear music and people singing. Perhaps I should have made my presence known to some of those people. Now they were all inside. I was pondering what my next move would be, when I heard voices and footsteps hurriedly coming up the walk! Grasping what might be my last chance, I decided to call out to them and make my presence known. There were two very kind looking ladies approaching. As their feet plied the steps, near the spot where I crouched, I gave my best appealing *Meeow --- Meeow!* At the same time I raised up my body to fully disclose my whereabouts. The two ladies stopped mid-way up the steps. I knew then that I, indeed, had delivered the very best meows of my entire life. They peered down at me. One of them exclaimed, "Oh, you poor little kitty!" The other lady joined in, sounding just as sympathetic, "Where did *you* come from?" After some words of endearment directed towards me, a discussion took place between the two ladies. A decision was made. The one lady, named Diana, reached down for me. Her demeanor and words were so comforting and reassuring, I all but fell into her arms. She carried me over to one of the mechanical monsters. The other lady got behind the wheel and we drove away. We traveled a short distance down the road, then turned on to a driveway at a farm with many fine buildings. I immediately found myself being whisked into a huge red barn. The other lady, named Idabelle, seemed to be in charge here. She opened a big sliding door on the side of the barn. With a few kind words of reassurance, I was released from kind lady Diana's arms into the barn. Then, they quickly closed the door behind them and were gone. I think they had to hurry because, having taken time for me, they knew they were going to be late.

I had found myself in a strange place, but certainly better than being left alone in a gravel field amidst a gathering of mechanical monsters! A feeling of calm came over me. I felt hungry. A few steps away were several dishes, not unlike the one I had eaten delicious fish from so very early this morning, although it seemed an eternity ago. I investigated and found one container still had some milk in it. No one was around, so I drank my fill. It was close to noon by then, and I was exhausted from my ordeal. I still seemed to be alone. I soon found a nice place in a pile of straw to nap and to dream of pleasant days ahead.

4

New Acquaintances

I awakened with a half-jump-start. How else could one awaken from a deep and sound sleep on a comfy bed of straw? I was aware that my privacy had been invaded. Whiskers had brushed my head as the stranger had come close for an inquisitive sniff. Raising up, I came eye to eye with this stranger -- a large orange cat. I presumed this was his domain. Certainly I was then a transient intruder, more or less. I decided to back away and we continued to eye each other. I suppose it was a matter of both domain and curiosity, an act of mutual examination. Whatever, it resulted in a recognition of something kindred in our spirits. But, he seemed to become bored and moved gracefully off out of sight.

Soon, I was to learn that there would be many cats of various colors using the barn as their home. Two of these cats were black, like me. They had the same characteristics as I did, except one had a shorter body and a larger, rounded head. Actually, my head is small for the size of my body, but, the lady soon to be my Ma, thinks I have a *big head* sometimes. Oops, I just *let the cat out of the bag* as to who was to be my new mom. The other was

17

slim in body, having a distinctive swing to his hind quarters, almost to suggest a swagger. Perhaps he had been injured by a mechanical monster in his youth, leaving him with this unique walk. These features made it easy to distinguish each of us, one from the other, but, all three of us were fine specimens, our smooth coats of black fur to be envied by the rest of the cat world.

I was to learn, and thankfully so, that most of the barn cats had congenial dispositions. I had not been in my new surroundings for a long enough period of time, nor had I gained enough confidence to feel qualified to assert any show of aggression and so, when our paths crossed, I considered them rivals who were best to avoid, if possible. But, the barn was so very huge and it pleased me to stroll throughout its spaces and it would take me hours to explore its many nooks and crannies. I learned that the barn was on the farm of the Berg family, and this old barn was affectionately known as the Berg Barn. With my new surroundings to explore, I all but forgot the betrayal by poor Old Man and Old Woman.

The inner section of the barn, huge in its expanse, was virtually a gym. There was bale after bale of straw or hay on which to jump. Sometimes I would miss my target and plummet to a thick layer of straw on the barn floor. That was great fun! There was discarded lumber in a huge pile, great to meander about and great to sharpen my claws! A large ladder, placed to ascend to the upper mow, provided a challenge to the bravest, for it took a certain acquired adeptness to master the small rungs of the ladder. Curiosity as to what was in the upper mow provoked many of us to test our skill at this adventure.

There had been two milking parlors, one in each end of the barn. No longer used, due to the retirement of the man of the house, they had been converted into living quarters for the cats. One was used as a sleeping section and the lady of the house had furnished it with individual cardboard boxes, lined with straw for warmth, and these were used as our beds. The other was used as our dining area. Here the lady of the house again showed her love for all of us. For in this section she provided ample containers, keeping them clean and always filled with food and drink. We also had a very long dinner plate made of a 3-foot wide strip of linoleum, marble in color, on which the lady would spread out our food. "Big," you say? Yes, it was big, probably 12-foot long, but remember it had to accommodate up to *seventeen* of us at one time! The food was good and plentiful. Sometimes, she would mix a small amount of special tid-bits into our regular food. Then, what a commotion we all would make as we dashed to get to the dinner table and vied for those special treats.

The lady of whom I speak is one of the nice ladies who had rescued me from the church yard. She came to the barn twice a day, morning and evening, to feed us. If she were a little off her usual time schedule, some of the felines would go up to the house, perhaps to hurry up their meal. They would wait at the back door, until she was ready and then escort her back to the barn. The others would stand on the stacked bales of straw and peer out the barn windows, anxiously awaiting their forthcoming meal.

Although I was quite content in my barn home, getting along very well with my feline friends, I felt the lady of the house had her eye on me, for she seemed to give me more attention and love than the others. Of course, I didn't complain about this! In fact I relished it. I would always return her affection, being sure to rub against her legs, in return, to show my affection, too. It became very clear to me, as I lived there on the lovely olde farm, that this lady was compelled by compassion to befriend abandoned cats. I could sense a special attraction between the lady and me, as though I somehow represented in a more direct way, all the abandoned cats she had saved from a terrible fate. Since she seemed to be evaluating me, especially my temperament, I remained very polite and was very careful to be on my best behavior whenever in her company.

After I had been a resident of the barn for about two weeks, the lady of the house, after giving me an especially warm greeting one morning, affectionately called me to her side. I didn't hesitate. Then, she gathered me up in her arms and carried me to the big white house, where she lived with her husband, the man of the house. Introductions were made and henceforth, they were to become my Ma and my Pa. Because I appeared to have such an especially glossy and silky-smooth coat of fur, I was officially dubbed with a middle name, "Ice." So, I was known from then on as Blackie "Ice" Berg. I liked the nickname because it made me think of myself as a kind of cool detective type, a kind of smooth and slippery sleuth. And, some of the other cats seemed to like to call me "Ice." Besides, in my new home, I really did feel pretty "cool." Now, I was truly a member of the Berg household, and felt that I had, at last, found a home of my own.

I was left to investigate my new basement quarters, while Ma fixed me a special dish of food to help me feel more welcome. With a quick glance, I could see my quarters were quite luxurious, what with carpet pieces throughout the basement floor, curtains on the windows, two sleeping beds, one for cold weather and one for warm weather, porcelain water and food dishes, and, best of all, my own separate bathroom. I had to thoroughly *case the joint*, as they say. Just kidding! Shame on me. I was really looking for clues that might suggest my new home would be less than permanent. I'll tell you like it is. I was still a little apprehensive, since it occurred to me that these great accommodations might only be temporary. And, I wondered if I could live up to Ma's expectations.

The next day Ma explained the routine of the household and explained very carefully to me just where I fit in. My special quarters seemed to me to be a place of supreme elegance. I often thereafter referred to them as my *apartment*. But, I admit, depending on my mood, or what was taking place there, I later sometimes simply called my quarters the *basement*, or the *cellar*. She again explained that I was to answer always to the name of Blackie, not Ice, as soon as I was called. It was then, really, that all my fears were put to rest. I silently said to myself, "*I see*," and I knew then that the welcome mat had been rolled out officially for me and I was at last in my *permanent* home! Silently I thanked Ma. I also hoped I could now presume some favors ... like asking Ma if Diana, who had also befriended me, could be my official God-Ma.

Knock, knock!
Who's there?
Yes ... Doctor.
Doctor Who?
Right again. I'm the Doctor Who
Who's here to needle you!!

5

A Visit to the Veterinarian

$\mathcal{T}$he days went by quickly. I enjoyed my life in the big white house. Things seemed to be progressing smoothly, until one infamous morning, during which there seemed to be an unusual amount of activity. Ma was looking for something. What she found was an oblong case with handles and little holes around the sides.

I was hungry. Ma had not given me my usual breakfast that morning. While I was pondering the condition of my stomach, Ma did a very strange thing. I watched as she went to my bathroom. She carried a small brown paper bag. When she returned, I could see that she had put something into the brown bag, for it now looked like a full lunch bag, except I had the odd intimation that it was not filled with fish sandwiches. Then, she put the brown paper bag into a carrier slot at the back of the oblong case. Before I knew what was happening, she had me in her arms and was stuffing me into that oblong case. What was going on here? I sure didn't want to end up anywhere near that brown bag! I resisted, out of pure instinct, of course, but

22

she was firm. The lid of the case closed down over me. I could turn around in the case; there was plenty of room, but I felt a little bit cramped.

Pa had moved the mechanical monster close to the house. Ma carted me out the door. I jostled from one side of the case to the other, feeling very much like a bag of bones. Twice, that brown bag almost bounced out of the slot and I thought it might slide into the case with me. Finally, I was placed on the seat between Ma and Pa, and everything seemed to stabilize. I looked over at the brown bag. I couldn't smell any food, so I knew we weren't going on a picnic. I wished we were, as my stomach growled. Then I thought that perhaps my nightmare was starting all over again, my thoughts went back to that time, not too long ago, when poor Old Man and Old Woman had taken me on a similar ride. I feared I was going to be abandoned again in some vacant parking lot beside a church, or worse. But, Ma and Pa seemed to be very fond of me, so I quickly got rid of those unpleasant thoughts. It didn't seem to me to be likely that they would abandon me now. Still, I couldn't figure out why I had not been fed. In spite of my intimations, my gaze again rested curiously on the brown paper bag. I soon discovered how much of a picnic this trip was *not* going to be for me!

The mechanical monster began to slow down. Suddenly, it stopped. We had arrived at our destination. Pa waited outside while Ma carted me into the building where we were greeted kindly at the door of an inner office. Then we were ushered into a small room. I was placed on a very cold, shiny metal table. Ma kept assuring me that I would be all right. Easy for her to say! It turned out to be my first trip to the veterinarian!

I was so uneasy about what was going on, or what was about to go on, that I squirmed until Ma stroked my back, managing to settle me down a bit. But, let me tell you, when the Vet and the nurse entered the room I figured *my goose was cooked.* Poked and prodded, with my skin rolled around, I thought they must be looking for a golden egg or a loose silver feather, or two! Thank goodness, Ma explained to me what they were doing. They were just looking for lumps, checking my ears for mites, weighing me, and generally assessing my health.

I was very tempted to grab one of those instruments they were using, so as to defend myself. Then, just as I figured it was all over, no harm done, the Vet came back into the room. All I saw was a long needle. "Hypodermic," Ma explained. Before I could scream out a *meoow*!, I was watching my own blood flow into that hypodermic monster! Imagine all this without my permission!

I was mulling over all these indignities, when again without my permission, they did a procedure that Ma called *taking your temperature.* Right in front of Ma! I figured I'd give them a temperature all right, say about 800 degrees! I felt like a volcano about to erupt! Withdrawing the *rod* from my backside, the Vet turned to the nurse, who had been calmly recording all the statistics, and pronounced, "Normal." While I tried to calm myself, the Vet turned to Ma and remarked that I seemed to be in excellent condition, though a bit ornery. I thought, "Who wouldn't be!?" Then the nurse said that the results of the blood sample and stool test, something that Ma called a *brown bag test,* would be available the next day. It was finally clear to me now what the brown bag was all about!

I didn't know it then, but I was to be subjected to these same indignities every year from then on! The examination seemed to be completed and I uttered a sigh of relief. I had to admit that it had not been so bad, after all. The Vet treated me with respect, giving me many reassurances and gestures of kindness. Actually, the Vet displayed great dexterity, if I may say so, and always stopped short of causing me any pain. Of course, the nurse had a nice, sweet way about her; very reassuring, and, she sure was pretty.

Just when I figured we were *out of there* and homeward bound, that there was nothing more they needed of me, the good Vet said, "You can pick him up in the morning." I thought then that they had something more dire in mind for me that evening. Whatever it was, it was obvious they weren't through with me yet! How could I have known that the real reason Ma brought me had not yet occurred. Ma patted me on the head. "Now you be a good boy. I'll see you tomorrow." She looked a bit concerned about me. Then she left, although with a hint of reluctance, I thought.

The sweet nurse carried me to a metal cage. She gently put me in, then placed a bowl of water by my side. "Be a good kitty," she said. She must have been kidding; who could get into any trouble in that cage! She left, only to return a few minutes later. She held another one of those hypodermic monsters. She got me good. Soon, I fell into a deep induced sleep. I was out of this world, enjoying the planetary nebula for I don't know how long. Later, I found out from Ma that I had been *given the works*, so I could become a gentleman cat - something called neutering. All I remember is that when I woke up I had a *care-less* sense of well-being. And, I was hungry!

The sweet nurse soon became a real honey to my eyes. She brought me a piece of fish that made me swoon as I sunk my teeth into it! I recall thinking that I had not enjoyed a meal so much since eating the fish Old Woman had given me the fateful morning when I had been carted off and abandoned. With a full stomach, and quite ex-hausted, I soon fell into a normal slumber to have happy dreams of seeing Ma and Pa in the morning.

Morning came quickly, and with it wonderful, beautiful Ma! She came early for me. I think she must have been as anxious to take me home as I was to go. I was placed gingerly into the carrying case and, bidding our good-byes, we were on our way. Even mechanical monster seemed friendly that morning. It gave off a pleasant purr as Pa put the *pedal to the metal.*

Peaking through the holes in my carrying case and out the car window, I could see the beautiful tree tops, alternating with the telephone poles against the skyline, as we journeyed down the road. They never before had looked so beautiful, maybe because I had never really looked at them. It always amazes me how beauty can be found in the simplest and most unexpected places. We just have to take the time to really look. In a happy anticipation of arriving home, I vowed that I would climb every tree, and I'd sharpen my claws on every telephone pole, just to express my happiness. At last we reached the farm. As I was released from the case, I surveyed my familiar surroundings. I remember thinking then that, once again, all seemed right in my world and I was happy!

The next day the Vet called Ma to report that the feline leukemia test results and the fecal test results were negative. That was a big relief to Ma, and when she explained to me that feline leukemia was fairly common in cats like us and that we could die from it, the good news from the test became a real relief to me, also.

It was much later, when Ma finally had the strength of spirit to carefully explain to me why she had been especially concerned about feline leukemia. She still had the heartache of losing her previous cat, Pritty Kitty, to the disease. One cold February day, Ma had seen a very pathetic sight, a wet, hungry, thin and frightened cat. It was hunched and shivering, out by the old garage, near the road, a convenient place for uncaring, cruel people to drop off unwanted cats. Ma could not just look away, and could not ignore its deplorable condition. She had brought it into the white house, dried it off with a warm towel and given it some milk. After just a few days, with special care, Kitty appeared to be much improved. He was a beautiful silver gray with green eyes. Ma wanted to adopt him, so she made arrangements for him to see the Vet. Pritty Kitty was checked over very carefully and, being a drop-off, also tested for leukemia.

It was discovered that Kitty was in the advanced stages of the disease. Shots would not help him. Ma had decided to keep him in the house, where he could be watched closely and be kept as comfortable as possible. He lived long enough for Ma to get attached to him. When he finally died from that awful disease it was a very sad day. The weeks and months after were very lonesome for Ma. The Vet had told Ma that Kitty was a Maine Coon Cat, a very sturdy and nice breed of cat. Had his previous owner done the right thing, that beautiful cat could have lived and given someone many years of wonderful companionship. After Ma told me about Pritty Kitty, I understood why she was so concerned about me. I also understood why she brought me into the big white house to stay with her. I resolved to make sure that I expressed my love for Ma as much as I could, knowing I could never take the place of Pritty Kitty. Actually, Ma never expected me to be anyone other than me.

In looking back, though we should not,
Recalling joys of loves we've not forgot,
We may so despair o'er joys we miss,
We lose the joys our future promises.

6

The Reunion

$\mathcal{D}$ays went by and life was good to me. Many times Ma, upon letting me out doors would call after me, saying, "Have a good time," or, "Have fun." Since my visit to the Vet, I had no driving interest in girl felines, but sometimes, for a frolic, I'd fancy one to chase. What a joy! So I chased the ladies whenever I felt like it. But, I had even more fun exploring the wide world of the farm, catching field mice and scaring birds.

I had not been into the barn for some time and, as a reward for having been particularly good lately, Ma invited me to go along with her one day when she fed the barn cats. That day I was to have the surprise of my life! With Ma carrying her standard menu of food, we proceeded to the barn. As usual, I waited outside while she spread the food on the linoleum dinner table. I never entered the barn at feeding time, but would busy myself nearby, investigating smells and movements around the area, until Ma was ready to return to the house. But this morning something was drawing, rather compelling me, to look in at the feeding cats. I walked to the threshold and immediately sensed a strong bond of familiar kinship.

Looking carefully at the bent heads of the numerous feeding cats, I was startled to see two new figures, side by side, who looked very familiar. Was it possible? I gave a loud *meow* and the two heads popped up in my direction. Brother Bo! And sister Fluff! There they were! They recognized me immediately, too. They leaped to my side. Our emotions in that moment were electrifying. My heart was bursting with joy. Here we were, together after so long a time! True, we were each older and more mature, but being reunited, it seemed like our youth was renewed. We rubbed against each other and displayed a camaraderie that was obviously family to any observer. Ma watched amazed. She easily had guessed the relationship. She later told me that she had found the two, frightened and hungry, huddled together out by the old garage near the road, one dark gray day a few weeks ago. She had brought them to the sanctuary of the Berg barn, under much the same conditions as my rescue by Ma from the church parking lot months ago.

I was sure that Bo and Fluff had endured some harrowing times before their rescue. They later told me of their daring escape from a strange institution. They had been severely tested, but they *had* endured. They had stuck together and now were safe in the custody of Ma and Pa. After spending some time together, Bo and Fluff returned to their meal and new friends in the barn, but not before I got Ma's permission to visit them on a regular basis, which she understandingly agreed to. I returned to the big white house that day, knowing that I had found my long lost brother and sister. I looked forward to sharing many happy times again with Bo and Fluff.

So much depends upon our barrow perspective,
Value decreed by the context in which we see.
Given this, how can we ever be sure we give
Of ourselves all we can give to be all we can be?

7

The Red Wheelbarrow

$\mathcal{O}$ne day as I wandered outside, making my daily inspection of the grounds, I heard a clinkety-clank noise close by. I looked in the direction of the sound and saw a neighbor pushing a rickety red wheelbarrow. The contents clanged together in the metal bin as he pushed the red contraption over the rough ground. Taking no chances that I might be added to his *collection*, I quickly ducked behind the nearby tulip bed. Ma told me later that he was collecting junk for the weekly trash pick-up.

In a half-crouched position, I tried to keep out of sight, yet tried to keep track of the man and his wheelbarrow. I moved my head this way and that; it was difficult to be subtle as I peered back and forth, first through the tall tulips, then around the edge of the bed. The man stopped several times along the way. I imagined he looked my way, but he had stopped only to pick something up. Each time he set the red wheelbarrow down on the ground, I heard a strange accentuated clank as the clinkety-clank sound stopped abruptly. How curious! Straining to see without being seen, I watched as he continued on his way. I watched a little longer, to make sure he did not change his course and head in my direction.

Finally, he passed out of sight and gradually the strange clinkety-clank sound subsided into silence. Only then was I satisfied that he was no longer a threat to me. Ma had been standing at the kitchen sink, washing dishes. It turns out she saw everything. She could plainly see me out the window as I ducked back and forth behind the tulips. She chuckled when she recalled to me later, how *cute* I looked while I was so busy trying to keep track of the man and his red wheelbarrow. Cute? Boy, did my face turn red! I didn't think there was anything cute about that episode at all. But Ma did spare me some deeper embarrassment. She never mentioned that she saw me destroy several of her tulips while I was ducking back and forth and she never laughed at how I had gotten into a sneezing frenzy from brushing my nose against the pollen in the tulip blooms. I remember how my sneezing almost gave me away as I monitored the movement of the man and his red wheelbarrow. When I asked Ma what the man was collecting and why was the wheelbarrow red and why was it called a wheelbarrow, she just laughed. She told me that as for the color of the wheelbarrow, it all had something to do with its sound, and that I'd have to study some poetry for an answer. As for the name, she explained that it is called a wheelbarrow because it has only one wheel and needed to *barrow* another! Cute.

I would defend in danger what I love
My strength to do so comes from above.
Whence truth and trust gain actual powers
To overcome the painful trials of trying hours.

8

The Pretty Red Gloves

What a beautiful sunny spring morning! I thought the weather could not have been more perfect. The temperature was around fifty degrees. A little cool, but just the way I liked it --- invigorating. It made me feel quite frisky.

Not far from the back door, my natural hunting expertise alerted me to a chubby chipmunk. It was almost impossible for me to resist chasing anything that moved. Instinctively, I stalked towards the chipmunk. But he spotted me in my tiger-like crouch and dashed off into the tall grass of the field nearby. I rarely felt like hunting anyway, especially this early in the morning. I admit that there were times I did set out to hunt, but to be truthful, my catnip toy was a much more pleasurable activity, and I had become accustomed to a nice big meal of Ma's personally served cat food, which was always easier to catch. It might seem that I was fighting my own nature when I refused to hunt simply for fun. As I grew older, my philosophy was becoming more and more one of *live and let live.*

I moved farther out in the yard. It was not long before I came across a small snake. There was no challenge here, for he had just crawled out from his Winter hibernation nook to warm himself in the sun. He was still too cold and sluggish to maneuver his body quickly enough to escape my *clutcherous* claws. Talk about wiggling! I held him awkwardly. Ever try to hold a slimy worm in your fingers? But, despite his wiggling, I successfully carried it up to the backdoor, and --- you guessed it --- right to Ma!

Nearby, I met Whitey and Whisper, two of the barn cats. They congratulated me and appraised my catch, much to Mr. Snake's chagrin, I'm sure. I placed it in the best location to surprise Ma when she came out the door.

Whitey and Whisper wandered off. I know they were thinking that I was being cruel to Ma for the surprise I'd left for her to find. But, it was one way to *keep her on her toes!* With that thought, I sauntered off to find a warm place to lay in the sun. I didn't go far away, though, because I wanted to be sure I could hear Ma when she came out the back door. Before I was even stretched out and settled, I heard the back door open, immediately followed by a scream, "*Blackieeee, not again?!*"

Why she always reacted this way, I'll never fully understand. I could only hope that one of these times, when I brought her a trophy, she would be pleased --- no, thrilled. Well, she was thrilled today; but, again, not quite in the sense I wished.

Perhaps, in time, I'd *mend my ways* and forget this trophy business. Then I would become Ma's *purr-fect* feline. (Ma and I would often chuckle about words which could be adapted easily to a language just for cats. I seem to recall in this instance that she wanted to get the *cat* out of *cat-tas-trophy*.) In any event, I resolved to become a better philosopher, since I was surely not interested in being a great wild life hunter, or in annoying Ma much more.

34

She recovered quickly, realizing the snake was no threat, and re-entered the house to fetch her usual implements of disposal, a dustpan and a broom. She carried the snake on the dustpan, taking it far out back, and gently let it slip off the pan into the tall grass, noticing a promising movement of renewed vigor in Mr. Snake. Ma was hopeful (she told me later) that Mr. Snake would recover to live a good snake's life, but *please*, far away from the house and yard. So much for my trophy for Ma!

She re-entered the house to put away her trophy-disposal tools, and I settled back down to enjoy the sunshine. It was not long before she came back out, and I noticed she paused, looking around suspiciously. For what, I wondered. Could she possible think I had time to catch another trophy and put it at the back door again? Finding the way clear, she headed for the henhouse. The henhouse, no longer used to house chickens, was now the place where Ma stored her gardening tools. Of course, she wore her proverbial big boots, and clutched a pair of pretty red gloves in her hands. The red work-gloves had to be new, for I had not seen them before. She removed a suitable rake and a large cardboard box from the henhouse. Thus equipped, she proceeded to the garden.

Ma usually did not wear gloves when she worked outside. She said they hampered her in her work. Confidentially, I think she liked the feel of the good earth between her fingers. She wore them today, I guess, to keep her hands presentable for some social function coming up; or, perhaps, because they were new and she wanted to properly initiate them!

I had found a nice comfortable place to nap close to the garden; but, I did not nap. I became too curious about what Ma was going to do in the garden. She commenced to rake up the debris that had accumulated during the winter, so the soil could be plowed and readied for the spring garden planting. I watched quite intently, in case a rodent might be uncovered from its winter hibernation and I could *go into action* and really help Ma *clean up* the garden!

She worked diligently, raking and filling the big cardboard box with the dry garden debris. She made many trips, dumping the contents she had collected onto the burn pile. Each time, the dry debris ignited fairly quickly in the smoldering pile left from the previous dump.

I had not seen a single rodent to chase after, and I soon became bored. I did observe, as I sat basking in the sun, that Ma was tiring, and thought of suggesting that she leave some of the work for tomorrow. But, *no-one* told Ma when to quit, except Ma herself!

She collected yet another box of debris and trudged over to the burn pile. It seemed as though she had read my mind, because, after emptying the box, she tossed it away from her. Her action indicated to me that she was finally going to quit for today. As she tossed the box, I noticed that one of her red gloves had gotten caught on the rough edge of the box. Then it fell off, dropping to the side, as the box came to rest on the ground. A breeze then blew a few leaves away from the pile. As Ma picked up the rake, she noticed that she was wearing only one red glove. She muttered something under her breath that sounded very strange to me --- something like, "*For eet's sake!*" She immediately dropped the rake and commenced rummaging through the debris that she had just dumped on the pile.

I was sure that the smoldering pile was about to burst into flames. Fearing for Ma's safety, I jumped up and raced to her side, hurdling through several still dormant perennial flower beds. Reaching her side, I tried to tell her to *back off* or she would get burnt. But, she turned toward me, saying, "But Blackie, I've lost one of my pretty red gloves." Before I could tell her where it was, she admonished me, saying, "Stay back, the fire could be dangerous!" I heeded Ma's warning and stepped back from the pile. It seems she was just as fearful for my safety as I was for her's! Ma's face was now colored in a fiery red glow, partly from frustration, but mostly from the heat of the now-bursting flames.

Seeing her condition, I excitedly rushed back to her side to try to tell her where her glove was. But, once more, before I could say a word, she pushed me away. She continued her frenzied search in an attempt to save her glove from the hungry flames. Even with *her* dogged determination, she could not find what was not there! I wondered how I could draw Ma's attention to the glove laying by the side of the box. As I considered what I could do, I was suddenly distracted by the smell of rubber. It was Ma's boots! She had stood too long in the hot ashes at the edge of the pile and they were starting to burn! Was she sacrificing her boots, and taking a chance on her own meltdown, for a single glove, pretty red as it might be?

The situation was worsening. I had to do some-thing! Suddenly, I had a brilliant idea. Because Ma was so concerned for my safety, I would skirt as close to the fire as I could, then move quickly toward the box, with the hope she would follow me with her eyes and see the glove. It would be risky, going so close to the flames. I'd have to be very careful I didn't catch on fire! But it was worth the risk. So. I took off. Ma's gaze followed me only half the way. Holy cats! I figured I'd have to do it again, only this time *closer*! But, luckily, Ma had smelled the burning rubber, too.

Realizing that her boots were beginning to smolder, she moved back from the fire, which by now was shooting flames into the air. Resigned to the likelihood that her glove had been consumed in the fire, she stooped to assess the damage to her boots. In doing so, she tottered back-wards towards the cardboard box. She was obviously

37

fatigued and she caught herself from falling with the help of her right hand, which miraculously touched the ground right where her other glove lay! I heard her exclaim, "For *Pete's* sake!" She had seen her pretty red glove, unrumpled and unscathed, waiting to be claimed. She was obviously pleasantly surprised, and as she looked in my direction, she completed her exclamation, "There you are!"

At first, I thought I had a new name, because her exclamation seemed to have been directed at me. But then she added, "Look Blackie, I've found my glove!" OK, that was fine; but, somewhat disconcerted, I had to ask her, "*Who* is *Pete*?" Ma laughed as she replied to my question. She said I'd have to wait and she would explain it to me at our next English lesson. For now, she just wanted to go in, wash up, and rest.

It had been a fatiguing day for me, too, if not physically, certainly mentally. So, I tagged along with Ma as she walked to the house in her smelly rubber boots. But, she had a smile on her face as she happily carried her two, now well-initiated, red gloves. On the way to the house, a most amazing and puzzling coincidence occurred. Just off our path, to the right of us, I spotted a small snake. It looked exactly like the fellow I had so arrogantly tried to surprise Ma with earlier that day. It did not move away. Its head was lifted high and its back was arched in a kind of question mark. I was amazed and very much puzzled to see that the snake held a dry red leaf in its mouth, almost as though wishing to present it to Ma! Ma was so fatigued that she never saw the snake, and I decided to wait until I had figured out just what it was that I had seen before telling her about it.

The next day, as I lay cozy and comfortable on top of the washer in my apartment, I wondered why yesterday I had not simply picked the glove up in my mouth and carried it over to Ma. She would have seen it immediately, eliminating all her frenzied frustration of trying to find it in the dangerously burning debris. The fact that I didn't, I think, has to do with something in my nature. Take dogs. Dogs are very good at such things, but dogs and cats rarely see eye to eye, let alone act like one another. Maybe I was thinking, subconsciously, that I didn't want to emulate, of all things, a dog *fetching*! Oh, well. Maybe *Pete* is the name of that loud, forever-barking dog who lives down the road from us!

Fe Fi Fo Fum, Happy are we tho' stuck on a rolling sea
On a windy raft of sticks stuck together with bubbly gum!
Fe Fi Fo Fum, Half-full, by far, far better 'tis here to be,
Than stuck like a cork in a bobbing bottle half-empty of rum!

9

The Basement Flood

*I*t was just like in the movies: Early one evening, while half dozing on the backdoor ledge, I heard a sudden strange noise. The sound of an explosive burst, a kind of *poof-phisht*, woke me up. I could hear a continuous spurting sound, like catsup suddenly releasing from a catsup bottle. Oh, maybe I shouldn't say *cat-sup*. Anyway, I listened for a while as the sound continued. Curiosity soon got the best of me. Curiosity never kills a cat, you know; it's what comes *after* curiosity that does all the damage.

I jumped from the ledge to the floor and crept in the direction of the sound. As I got closer, I became aware that my paws were getting wet. I hesitated, for then I was approaching rivulets of water. Yes, rivulets. Glancing to one side, towards the sound, I saw the source of the trouble: Water was spurting from a hole in a defective hose attached to the water tank. The floor was filling fast with water and, determining immediate action was necessary, I entered the wet zone. Quickly, my feet sopping in the danger zone, I jumped to the top of the ping-pong table, a good island of safety, I thought.

But, the floor was becoming inundated, literally. Why didn't Ma or Pa come and take care of this catastrophe? It finally dawned on me that they knew nothing about the fast-becoming crisis. I hung my head over the edge of the ping-pong table to assess the situation, only to see my favorite toy go floating by. It was the artificial mouse Aunt Vivian had brought out to me on one of her many visits to see Ma and Pa. Aunt Vivian was usually very nice to me, often inquiring as to my health. But, you know I've got to say this with my *tongue in cheek*, for, more often than not, she would tease me unmercifully, either pinching me or pulling my tail or just plain rough-housing. Sometimes she'd even pick on me for not waxing, or combing, my hair down properly. Of course, I didn't let her know it, but I rather enjoyed Aunt Vivian's teasing. I think I always did like to be the center of attention. Aunt Vivian likes to be a ham, too. I guess you could say, "Hams that play together, stay together." Come to think of it, strange she never accepted Ma's invitation for me to go home with her for a day or two. Do you suppose Ma was teasing us both?

Anyway, to get back to the disaster that was be-falling my territory, there were other articles journeying down the waterway below me. I saw a ping-pong ball bobbing along with an orange rubber ball. Somehow, they looked very similar to me as they bobbed up and down in the flow, and I recall thinking that disasters treat everyone and everything the same. I could see myself soon bobbing up and down, too. Funny how I then remembered that Ma had threatened to take them out to the barn for the other cats to play with, if I didn't play with them more. Looking off to the corner of the basement, I could see a hedgeball slowly losing its mooring. Soon it would be gobbled up in the main stream. Funny how you seem to remember odd little facts about this and that when you're in the middle of a mess. In the fall, Ma would gather up a quantity of these hedgeballs and place them strategically around the basement wall. The smell of them was supposed to drive away the big dirt spiders that were otherwise apt to come in. Ma couldn't tolerate these big spiders, but I always found them to be a great source of fascination and very entertaining. I think I ate one, once, when I was very young and inclined to act instinctively. As I recall, it wasn't too tasty. You know, it's hard for me to believe that a spider like that could have a better sense of smell than me. I never detected any *drive-away-the-spider* odor from those hedgeballs. I wondered if hedgeballs could swim better than spiders, too.

The situation was becoming critical. The water was getting deeper and deeper by the minute. Ma and Pa seemed the most likely source of help. They were my only real hope and I recall thinking then that, if they didn't hurry, they'd never get *this* cat out of *cat*astrophe! How could I alert them to my impending doom? I couldn't bark like a dog, nor nearly as loud. My fiercest meow would never be heard over the blare of the TV. I thought of jumping from the ping-pong table to the stair steps, thus reaching the landing where I could scratch loudly on the kitchen door. But the distance seemed far too great for me to risk it.

I glanced in the direction of my bathroom. A feeling of real dread entered my being. This was all too familiar a feeling. The litter pan was still there, but would it float and could I reach it? The moat between me and it was also too wide for me to jump across. Just then, I was distracted. The upstairs kitchen door opened. I could see Ma's feet enter the landing. She later told me that she was only checking to see if I was inside the house. She saw the ping-pong table, me, and the water all at the same time. She called out to Pa, "come here, quick!" She came down the steps toward me. When she reached the next to bottom step, I made a tremendous leap and landed right on her shoulder. I hung on as though my life depended on it. I really thought it did.

Pa put on his boots and waded through the water to where he could shut off the water pump. When he shut the valve, the water stopped leaking out. By this time, Ma had put her boots on, too. I could only watch as they cleaned up that nasty mess. I glanced over to my litter box, which somehow had escaped any damage. I used it two times before Ma and Pa finally got everything back to normal. You know, I did learn something valuable from that episode. A few days after the flood, Ma told me that the distance I finally jumped, from the ping-pong table to her shoulder, was almost twice as far as it was from the table to the bottom of the stair steps. Goes to show you that, if you trust the target for which you aim, its always possible for you to reach it.

There are so many places a cat would rather go,
Than out on a limb with a barking dog below!
Then how come so many cats end up in a tree
Quite far from all the places they'd rather be?

10

Up a Tree, Out on a Limb

Would you excuse me? I have to leave for a photo session with Ma. She wants me to pose on my favorite backdoor ledge, so she will have pictures of me to illustrate one of my stories. When I come back, I'll tell you the scary episode I had with a mongrel named Chew-Chow.

I liked my backdoor ledge. I thanked Pa many times for making it specially for me. In fact, I thanked him every time I jumped up on it to rest, or to view whatever was going on outside. Sometimes some very hostile activities took place right in front of me, but I was always safely out of harm's way while sitting on the ledge. I could see clearly, unless the window glass was totally frosted up, as sometimes happened in severe cold weather. Ma usually kept the window spotlessly clean for me.

Flash! I'm back. OK, now for the mongrel. One day, having left the security of my quarters to do a bit of exploring outside, I looked up to see a very large, very menacing dog, staring down at me. For Pete's sake! I was later to learn the dog's name was *Chew-Chow*. It was an appropriate name, considering his temperament. He was a notorious pooch who lived somewhere in the area. It seemed his only purpose in life was to terrorize all the cats around here. We must have seen each other at the same time; I had no doubt whatsoever regarding his intentions. We cats have a sense that way, you know, especially where dogs are involved. He sprang toward me as I took off for the nearest tree. I had to thank Ma, again. She didn't believe in having my nails clipped. Tell you truthfully, I needed every sharp claw for climbing that tree, as fast as I went up it. That dog was so close behind me that I swear I felt his hot breathing on my backside as I scrambled up. In no time, no, in *less than* no time, I reached the highest limb at the treetop. My heart was pounding. In my haste, I had gone out too far on the limb. This was certainly not my safe shelf. I shifted my weight and tried to get a better hold, but I felt the limb bend, then crack beneath me. As my heart began to pound a Susa march, I inched myself cautiously backwards to a sturdier part of the limb. I figured if I fell, it would be a fatal landing; if not fatal by the fall, then fatal by the dog.

Chew-Chow was in a frenzy on the ground below me. His barking was enough to drive a cow to stop chewing her cud. I tell you, that's awful loud! Having reached a safer and more comfortable place on the limb, I steeled myself to look down. Chew-chow was still acting totally out of his mind, barking wildly up at me as he leaned his two front paws menacingly against the tree trunk. At the time, it looked like he leaned half way up that tree. No way was he going to get any invitation from me to *come on up and see me sometime*. He was so close that, if he jumped again, I probably would have learned how to fly very quickly. Believe me, I would have had no problem climbing into the clouds and heading into the sunset.

True, Chew-Chow had me *up a tree*, and *out on a limb*, but I was still *high and dry* and by no means *down and out*. Need I say *any shelf in a storm*? It was a strange scene: Here was a cat clutching to the bark of a tree for dear life, while just below was a dog whose bark threatened to finish off a dear life. After a period of time somewhat akin to an eternity, his vicious barking ceased. I think he got a hoarse throat, if you want to know the truth. I realized I could outwait him, and, before long, he seemed to realize that, too. He started to lose interest, although he kept wagging his tail furiously. Doesn't a wagging tail indicate a continuing interest in the hunt? I figured anyone on the receiving end of that tail could get a powerful dose of whiplash. Finally, he calmed himself, and with a couple of last whiffs at the base of the tree trunk, lumbered off through our yard, in search, I'm sure, of some other unsuspecting cat. *There oughta be a law.*

When I sensed that all danger had passed, I crept carefully back along the limb until I reached the tree trunk. I remember thinking, as I crept along, that, if there ever was a next time --- mind you, I hoped there never would be --- but, if there ever was, I'd choose a better escape route. I cautioned myself to be careful and to not get overconfident on my descent. I had to inch my way down backwards. When I got close to the ground, I turned around and made a fine leap to the good old *terra firma.* I think I literally kissed the ground when I landed.

I'm glad Ma hadn't taken a picture of me up on *that* shelf! We later laughed about the episode as we studied some of the old clichés of the English language one rainy afternoon. Some old familiar sayings seem to stick like glue to old memories. And, that day I found out first hand, or more correctly by the seat of my pants, why hot air makes things rise!

When the sun sets into the deep dark night
Out come aliens and creepy crawly creatures
Who seem to glow in the dim moon light.
Look out! Look out to see their eirry features!

11

Creatures of the Night

$\mathcal{M}$ost times, Ma was very good about letting me in or out, especially whenever I stood at the door uttering an appealing, yet plaintive, *meow, meoow.* I remember one time, though, I had gone outdoors with Ma when she went to feed my barn cat friends their evening meal. Usually, I would come back in with her when she was finished. But that evening the crisp outdoors was especially inviting after a cleansing rain all afternoon. I decided to stay behind and roam about a bit to enjoy the freshness of the air.

Soon dusk came and lights were turned on in the house. I could see Ma moving around in the kitchen preparing supper. I was plainly visible to her through the kitchen window. I had decided it was time to come in, but she probably couldn't hear my usual I-want-to-come-in meow over the TV. Ma and Pa have a habit of watching TV while they eat supper. I sensed that they would soon be leaving the kitchen, so I let out one of my loudest meows. No reaction; the door didn't open. Soon after, the lights in the kitchen went out. Then Ma and Pa moved into the living room. It was evident to me that they were settling in for their usual quiet evening of *Wheel of Fortune* and *Jeopardy*. They had probably forgotten all about me.

I waited and waited. This waiting was really tiresome. I figured there was still some time left for me to go on the prowl, but then I couldn't risk not being close to the house when Ma's memory returned. I couldn't even watch birds to while away my time; they'd all gone to bed. The night was still, yet oddly noisy. I could hear many unseen night creatures singing their strange night songs. None-the-less, in a relaxed mood of awareness, I curled up on the step, leaving one ear cocked and one eye open. I dozed, half-waking whenever my head started to droop. I could hear rain drops dripping down from a faulty eave nearby. They fell with a methodical *plop...plop...plop*, making a muffled thud as they landed on a lily pad below. Soon I was fast asleep, my head nestled between my front paws.

A short time later, I was awakened by the somber hoot of an owl. It was perched on a branch of a nearby tree. I could feel his watchful eyes on me as they penetrated through the darkness. His proverbial "*hoot...hoot...hoot*," proclaimed a good question. It seemed to be saying to me "Who, who, who are you?" I shrugged my shoulders; what I'd like to know was, "*Who* was going to let me in!

Then a large possum sauntered by. It seemed to move lightly on its short stubby legs. It was going hither and thither, looking for something to eat. I figured he'd easily find some seed dropped from the bird feeder or a pear fallen from one of the pear trees in the back yard. It was too large a possum for the owl to attack. I could have taken him on, but I was in no mood for a confrontation. I just watched him as he ambled out of sight somewhere off in the night. I wondered where such creatures spend their daylight hours.

Shortly after the possum disappeared, all the lights in the house went off. It was clearly, I should say 'darkly,' evident to me that Ma and Pa had completely forgotten about me. I figured I'd have to spend the rest of the night outdoors. That's not something that normally bothers me, for actually I do like the deep dark hours of the night, but that night I really would rather have had a good sleep in my own bed. Oh, well; I prepared myself mentally for a "*Who-cares-night-out*." I curled up once more on the hard cold stone step. I was exhausted from all the anxious waiting and soon fell asleep again.

As soon as I started to sleep soundly, I was awakened by an extremely offensive odor. The smell was so strong it was actually disturbing. Even with my superior night vision, at first I could not see what it was. Finally, as it approached, I could see a white stripe down its long black body. There should have been no wondering about what animal it was. Instinctively, I knew I would never want to tangle with that fellow. The odor grew even stronger. It obviously had nowhere near the concern for self-hygiene that I had learned from my Mom-mew. I certainly wouldn't want to offend anyone, like this skunk offended me. I was about to leave in order to escape further offense when the fellow quietly turned away and faded back into the night. I was sure, I think, that I hadn't offended him. Somehow that skunk managed to linger nearby, long after it had ambled away!

Already, I had seen an owl, a possum, and a skunk. I was prepared to see a couple of bats, a raccoon or two, and even a fox. May as well see *the whole shebang*, I thought. I looked around; everything seemed ominously quiet. I looked up at the moon and the stars. The moon seemed to smile at me and the stars seemed to float like tiny spaceships. Then I thought about Ma and Pa watching TV. I wonder if they'd believe me if I told them tomorrow, when I --- of course --- expected to see them again, that I'd seen a flying saucer and little green creatures with laser flashlights tromping out in the oat field. Oh well. I've been reading too many fantastic comic books. My imagination was starting to get carried away, *abducted* maybe. Who knows where a cat goes at night anyway?

I was about to settle back down on the step for the rest of the night, when I heard the screen door slam. I turned my gaze to the house. I saw a light come on in the kitchen. Now, fully awake, I saw Ma open the sliding patio door. There she stood in her white nightgown, looking very much like an angel, welcoming me in. When I realized I was not dreaming, that she was really there, beckoning me in, I moved my stiff body to join her. When she reached down to stroke me, uttering apology after apology, to make amends for forgetting me, I turned my head to the side, exposing a section of my neck to her, so she could see where the *aliens* had implanted a probe. Oh, well.

Ma had not altogether forgotten me. As the saying goes, *better late than never*! I realized she probably had more things on her mind than I had on mine. I also took into consideration her age, since she was *slightly* older than me. So I stopped momentarily on my way down the stair steps to my apartment, glanced back at her and gave her a twitch of my tail. That was my way of saying *thank you*, and to show my forgiveness. I don't think she saw the probe. Oh, well. Like I said, "sometimes my imagination abducts me."

12

A Fragile Toy

I was up rather early. The day before, Rusty had commented that my climbing muscles in my shoulders were weak. We had been working out on the log pile by the barn. So today, I decided to work on my deltoids. I had finished my pushups and had begun to rotate my paws upward with the weights when Ma suddenly called me to get ready to go to the barn with her. She was getting ready to feed the cats. It was a damp and gloomy morning. A deep soaking rain had fallen all night long. Ma figured it would cheer everybody up if we went a little early to feed and visit with my barn friends. I especially wanted to visit awhile with Bo and Fluff.

Ma donned her rain cap, and off we tramped through the wet grass. On the way, we passed under a huge cottonwood tree. Its Latin name is *populus deltoides*. Never let an educated cat surprise you. Anyway, as we passed under the cottonwood, Ma felt a sudden wet-sounding *plop* on her cap. She said she knew what it was. It was just a dropping, a deposit from a fine feathered friend. She decided not to stop there to investigate, but went on with her mission to feed and visit our barn cat friends. She just chuckled and said she would clean it up when she got back to the house. So we continued on our way to the barn.

As always, some of the cats came to greet us and to enthuse over what might be the surprise morsel for them that day. Ma didn't disappoint them. She had brought melon rinds! The cats had acquired a taste for them and would always eat them first. Then they would turn their attention back to the commercial dry cat food Ma always served. I felt kind of superior that day, since I had eaten a breakfast of tuna. I waited patiently until all the cats were through eating. Then I mingled with them to discuss any news there might be. Bo and Fluff had no news to share with me. As they say, *no news is good news*. We laughed at a joke one of the cats whispered and Ma watched as we played tag for a while.

Finally, Ma finished her other chores in and around the barn. We then decided to leave. Some of the cats were ready for a mid-morning full-belly snooze anyway. Bo and Fluff headed for their favorite slumber spot in the straw as Ma and I started back to the house. As we entered the house, Ma removed her rain cap. The *plop* we had heard on her rain hat as we went out to the barn we heard again. Something went *plop* on the floor. We were both surprised. At first we thought it was one of those giant tomato worms. But that was silly, for big tomato worms do not climb trees.

Ma had not turned the light on yet. It was rather dim inside the house, so we didn't recognize what it was we were looking at. Then, when the light went on, we both laughed. We were relieved to see that this bird dropping or tomato worm was actually a soaked seed blossom from the cottonwood tree. Although this one was a big blossom --- at least five inches in length --- it was still light as a feather and the cottony fluff was already almost dry. Ma said these blossoms drop profusely for a short time in the spring. This one had targeted Ma and had become a hostage, wedged in a crease of her rain cap. It had stayed there the whole time she did her chores. Ma wondered out loud if the cotton fluff could be spun into thread to make a cozy little blanket for me. But I had other ideas. Inadvertently, Ma had brought in a new toy for me. I figured playing with a *populus deltoides* toy would be a perfect wrap-up to my earlier deltoid exercises. Alas, the toy proved too fragile in the paws of a cat with my deltoid power: A few left jabs, and it fell apart.

O hey, when my thick blood seems to quick,
And my heart begins to throb kind of weak,
It's time for this cat to head down to the creek,
Or say, is it creek, for those of eastern speak?

13

A Trek to the Creek

$\mathcal{B}$ad weather was forecast for tomorrow and the next day. Today was beautiful. I decided to take advantage of the rest of the day by inviting Bo and Fluff to accompany me on a trek to the creek. We could watch for frogs and all kinds of other interesting little creatures down there. So, I set off to look for Bo and Fluff.

On the way, I was distracted by a garter snake. It was headed in the direction of the creek, no doubt looking for water. Seeing me, it stopped. It must have hoped I'd not seen it. It took some exertion on my part to keep from chasing him down to the creek, but I decided to let him meander away uninterrupted. As I moved away, it showed its thanks by slithering a bit faster on its way. I figured I'd best get along to find Bo and Fluff before the day slipped away any further.

Continuing on my way, I came across two beautiful butterflies. I watched them hover over a clump of pink phlox. It was amazing to see them flutter to and fro around the blossoms. Still, I was in a very considerate mood. I decided not to intervene for some fun, and instead let them flutter away. I watched them closely, for they seemed romancing things; enthralled by a fall breeze, their wings moved back and forth, from this to that, in flit then flat in a fit of light fantastic dancing. Fancy that, *Mr. Shire*, now I'm almost a poet! Looking around, I thought I might see Bo and Fluff out enjoying the menagerie of the yard. But they were nowhere in sight, so I continued on my way to the big Berg barn.

The grass was lush and green. I stopped to nibble a blade or two. When I did, I came face to face, more accurately eyeball to eyeball, with a giant fat green worm! We looked at each other. That worm was probably as surprised to see me as I was to see it. The vegetable garden was nearby. I suspected this creature was a tomato worm, picked off a plant by a bird and dropped in the yard. It was lucky to be alive. I left it alone. It did not look the least bit appetizing anyway. In time, it would find its way back to the garden, and back to a tomato plant. Ma would probably find him there and fling him back here again; that is, if he made it back to the garden in the first place, what with all these feathered warriors about. Come to think of it, wasn't there a philosopher who once wrote about pushing a rock up a mountain, only to have it roll back down, only to be pushed back up again, only to roll back down and be pushed back up again, again and again? Who am I to repeat what he wrote? I think I was thinking too much. But I do think I was pretty smart in leaving that worm alone!

Near the barn is a large patch of clover from which Ma has picked, and kept in a neat collection, numerous four-leaf clovers. She has warned me, in my search for grass to eat, to be careful not to eat too many of this variety. She chuckled, as she explained that I wouldn't be able to handle *all that luck*! I decided to see if I could find a four-leaf clover. I looked over and over, over the patch, pushing some of the clover aside with my nose. I came close to sneezing a couple of times before I decided it would be best to leave all that luck to Ma. As I moved closer to the barn, I laughed as I thought of her warning. Though it wasn't quite voluntary, I was heeding her advice after all!

Finally, I reached the barn. Outside, by the door, Ma kept a pan filled with fresh water for the barn cats. I took a deep drink from it to fuel myself for the trek on down to the creek. I had just about quenched my thirst when I heard a deep voice yell, "*Hey, Ice!*" I looked up. It was old Rusty, one of my best barn friends. He had been watching me from a short distance away. I waved a paw to him and he came up to say hello and to talk. He told me that a family of raccoons had recently moved into the barn. Ma was now feeding them, too. Raccoons liked whatever was left-over from cooking. They also liked apples, potato peelings, and salad greens. They didn't eat too much of the barn cat's food, but they would if they were hungry enough. Ma had bought some commercial dog food for them. Rusty said that they seemed to like the dog food a lot. Rusty stuck his tongue out, "ugh!" Both of us snickered.

Rusty said he heard Ma say that the raccoons were messy eaters and none of the water dishes stayed clean for long. He said I was lucky to get a good clean drink when I did. The best time for us to get a drink was when Ma filled the water dishes, and the water was still fresh before the raccoons spilled it or messed it up. Ma thought she had outsmarted them when she put our water dish outside the barn door, but the raccoons eventually found it there, too.

Rusty explained that he'd just come back from the creek, otherwise he would have joined us. It sure was good talking to him, and the water was indeed refreshing. I remember thinking that it was a good thing raccoons really don't clean their food in water before they eat it. A cat would have to be mighty thirsty before it would drink water that tasted like dog food!

Where were Bo and Fluff? I looked in the resting area of the barn. I found Bo sound asleep in his cardboard box. I woke him up with a brotherly meow. He roused, stretched his back, arching it in a perfect semi-circle, climbed out of his box, and greeted me with a nuzzle to my face. He agreed to accompany me to the creek. I asked him where Fluff was. He had no idea, so we set out to find her.

Ma and Pa had two gardens, one East of the barn and the other, back of the house, the area I had already passed through. We decided to look around inside the big barn first. As we started, we came across the logs lined up against the wall of the inner mow. We decided to pause and sharpen our claws. I enjoyed coming out to the barn and joining Bo and the other cats in this activity. There was no place in my apartment that I could accomplish this, and Ma didn't appreciate my using the door casing at the kitchen door, which now carried deep grooves and was much in need of repair.

Bo and I worked those logs until we could cut glass with our claws. It was a tough work-out, too. We laughed at how we were sure our calisthenics would keep us from getting sand kicked in our faces. Really, this activity is helpful in strengthening our body muscles. As soon as we finished with the log-lifting, we continued our search for Fluff. We soon realized she was nowhere inside the barn. Bo then pointed to a short-cut out of the barn.

It was a small hole near the ground, no doubt made by woodchucks. It was just large enough for us to comfortably squeeze through. Another good test of our muscular dexterity's! As we emerged, we almost run into two young woodchucks. We watched them as they scampered and chased each other through the tall grass. Ma was always perplexed at how woodchucks could look so clean when they were always digging around in the dirt. Of course, she was referring to the woodchucks who had a habit of digging up the flower bed she'd worked so hard to establish. The flower garden occupied the ground area where an old garage had once stood. They were persistent wood-chucks, all right. Even when their cover had been blown, they would continue to dig, dig, dig. As fast as they would dig a hole, Ma would fill it back up. It had been a losing battle for Ma. She finally resigned herself to accepting one big hole right in the center of her flower bed!

Skirting the tall grass, our search took us toward the back east garden. In the garden we saw a splash of cream-colored fur. There was Fluff! As we approached we saw she was busy. She was crouched over something. When we got a little closer we saw what she was doing. Muskmelon! Fluff was so intent on her feast that she didn't even notice us as we approached. Ma would be surprised to learn who it was feasting on her beautiful ripe melons! But, I'm sure Fluff wasn't the only culprit raiding the melon patch. I'm sure of this because, just last year, we found a melon plant growing down by the creek. Some animal, maybe even one of us, had planted a seed. But Fluff had never gone down to the creek until earlier this year. The plant had grown quite well, since it could draw needed moisture from the creek. Ma had come across it by accident and was really surprised to find it growing there. It produced two nice juicy melons for Ma and Pa before someone else discovered it and raided all the other melons before they were ripe. Perhaps, this raider was Fluff. She had an insatiable appetite for them. This was easy for us to see, as we watched her feast on the melon in front of us.

Pointing to Fluff, I told Bo that there's *one* of the reasons Ma has stopped trying to grow any melons. Now, Ma goes to the market for them. You know what she does with the rinds. All the barn cats love melon rind served with their regular food. Melon rinds and cooked sweet potato skins were the favorites of all of us. Of course we also liked to feast on the *doggie bag* goodies Aunt Vivian would often bring out to us on her visits to Ma and Pa. When Fluff finally looked up and spotted us, there was nothing left of the melon. We greeted her warmly and told her about our plans to take a trek to the creek. Fluff thought that was a great idea and dashed off in front of us.

Just then, Ma came out of the house with a load of food for the supper meal. We all stopped in our tracks. I remember thinking, "Is it *that* late in the day, already?" (To this day, I don't know where that day went.) We quickly decided to postpone our *great trek* until the next good day.

Be it trickle crik, creek, or sea; upon its banks I break,
To flush a bully frog or fish my favorite lake,
To fetch a breakfast, sun upon a log, or take a skinny dip.
Thru hook, crook, burr, and slip, it's always worth the trip!

14

Trek Two to the Creek

*I*t rained for the next two days, solid. These were two dark days spent with my neighbor, Smiley, trying to translate the Latin verses of Catullus! Talk about vertigo, when the sun finally broke through on the third day, we all were primed to get down to the creek for sure this time! After breakfast, I ran out to the barn and joined up with Bo and Fluff. They were just as eager as me to get to the creek. Fluff said that two days confined with Rusty's old jokes was enough to drive her crazy.

We headed off in the direction of Fluff's melon garden. When we got there, we made sure that Fluff stayed between us, Bo on one side, me on the other. We weren't going to let her stay there and feast on another melon! The melon garden was not far from our destination, so once we cleared the garden, it didn't take us long to reach the creek. When we approached the edge of the creek, we were greeted with the sounds of *plop...plop...plop* as each big frog, startled by our sudden and silent arrival, leaped quickly into the safety of the clear, deep water. A dragon-fly, his reveries also disturbed by our sudden presence,

66

skimmed away just above the surface of the water. He moved too fast for us to chase him.

Frog plopping was always one of our favorite activities. In fact, I almost caught a frog. It must have been a bit lazy, or perhaps hard of hearing. He was dozing probably happily in the sun, for he never saw me, and never heard me, until I crouched just behind him. I took a swipe at him and just grazed his back leg as it stretched out in his panicked leap. I know it sounds cruel, but that is the nature of a cat. Maybe, if we all were human, we'd all be more compassionate toward each other and our fellow creatures. Don't you suppose? Really, I was kind of glad he got away. It is true, you know, most of the real thrill is in the chase, not in the catch. Anyway, he managed to escape intact. But, wouldn't you know it, I had leaned too far out over the water right behind him as he leaped out from the bank. *Plop*, he makes a beautiful dive, almost no splash, except for mine. I *splopped*, unceremoniously, in a kind of cannonball imitation, head first into the creek. I got so soaked I looked like I'd lost fifty pounds! The water wasn't all that bad. It was the mud. I floundered around and when I tried to climb back on the bank, I was so water-logged, I kept sliding back into the water. When I finally did clamber out onto dry land, Bo and Fluff were laughing so loud, that I shook myself extra hard, making sure some of the mud spattered off me in their direction.

It wasn't too long after my mud bath that we all realized we'd had it as far as frog plopping goes. There probably wasn't a frog sitting on a lily pad, let alone on either bank for fifty miles up or down that creek. We didn't need to take a vote, but if we had it would have been unanimous, three cats to none - and a hundred thousand frogs to zero - in favor of us heading back home.

On the way up from the creek, we spied the mulberry tree. It was located a short distance from the barn.

We decided to have a good frolic in it to round out the day. The tree was not very old and it was not very tall. Consequently, its branches were not too sturdy, in fact they were downright spindly. But, we had no fear of falling from it, so we raced each other to see who could climb to the top first. We reached the bottom of the tree together, practically colliding with each other. As we climbed up the small trunk, a scene of sheer pandemonium took place. We had disrupted a whole flock of birds. They had been feeding on the ripe mulberries. They flew off in a din, loudly proclaiming their objections to our invasion. Then they made a beautiful boomerang-turn in the air, shrieking all the while and, in one flock, circled overhead two or three times. You can imagine what we all looked like as we dodged all those bombs! You know, it's true: Never interrupt birds at their dinner table unless you are prepared to risk a bit of strafing and some scrappy fallout.

Fluff did not venture very high up in the tree. She stayed clear of the aerobatics (and aeroballistics) of the birds and left the higher technologies of acrobatics to Bo and I. She sat on a lower limb and sedately watched as Bo and I recklessly vied to outdo each other, as we literally flew from one branch to another. Actually it was more like we fell from branch to branch. Perhaps we were trying to imitate the squirrel, who just the other morning, hung from his back feet in order to reach down into the bird feeder for seeds. I know I should not have been deliberately climbing trees, especially after my experience on the broken branch which dangled precariously close to sweet old Chew-Chow. Thankfully, it was not Chew-Chow who drove me up this tree. And, I'd learned from my previous excursions into the mulberry that its branches would bend but not break. Anyway, Bo and I had great fun and teased Fluff about being too reserved to join in on our fun.

It was getting late. The birds were still scolding us from a short distance away. We decided to *call it a day*. We also knew that Ma would be coming out early to put some drops into Chelsea's and Mischief's ears. The Vet always had the perfect solution for ear mites. Ear mites were giving Chelsea and Mischief the fits. Chelsea especially, was rubbing herself raw with her ceaseless itching.

As we approached the barn, we saw that Ma had already come out of the house and was on her way to the barn with the medicine and the evening ration of food. We looked at each other and shrugged, thankful we'd decided to get down from the mulberry tree in time. Ma would never know what we'd been up to. But as Bo and I came into her view, she shouted, "Oh, oh, I know what you two have been up to!" I looked at Bo. Bo looked at me. Bo looked like he had the measles or something. Here and there, his fur was smeared with the scarlet stains of ripe mulberry. Bo told me later that he hadn't noticed until Ma shouted at me, "Blackie, whatever happened to *you*?" I must have looked very strange, indeed. I was a real *work of art*, covered as I was with cakes of mud *and* spatters of scarlet!

When I got back to the house, Ma had quite a time getting me cleaned up. I chose not to answer her when she asked again what had happened to me. I thought, *Tempus fugit, et tempus tacitus est*. Time flies, and time is silent. (Ma would have been happy to know I had learned Latin as a source of English. She probably would also be surprised to learn that I had become a Latin lover. Anyway, I knew enough now not to say anything!) I do remember her asking me if I wanted some catnip, and me answering quite willingly, quickly, and loudly, "Si, si!" That is a Latin *yes* or a statement decidedly to the affirmative. But my escapades of that day, the day of "trek two to (make that *trek into*) the creek," remained an *opus* mystery to Ma.

I'm Rick, I'm Pete! I never thought I'd be a star
Or wear a costume to make you wonder who I are!
As laughing children try to guess my new identity!
Trick or Treat! Oh, Ma...You know it's only me!

15

Ready for Halloween

One brisk October day, Ma came home from shopping, her arms full of packages. As she awkwardly opened the door, one of the packages slipped from her grasp and the contents dropped to the floor. Impulsively, I ran to investigate the piece of bright orange as it unrolled like a runner before me. Seemingly, an orange carpet had been rolled out just for me!

After unloading her other packages, Ma quickly stooped and retrieved the run-away piece of orange cloth. Noting my interest in it, she remarked, "Blackie, it *will* be yours all in good time." It wasn't until a few days later that I understood what she meant.

The next day, I noticed she had commenced to work on the pretty orange material. Equipped with scissors, thread and needle, she worked enthusiastically, glancing now and then in my direction with a measuring eye, contemplating if proportions were correct, as she fashioned each particular article. One piece, horizontally oblong, had two holes fashioned in it. To this already strange looking piece, she affixed to the rim a small artificial pumpkin which was mounted on thin, but sturdy, wire. I was almost hypnotized as I watched that little pumpkin sway provokingly back and forth.

Soon, all the pieces were completed and Ma summoned me for a *dress rehearsal*. I was curious about all this, so I cooperated as she placed and then tied an orange cape around my shoulders. To top it off, the two-hole apparel was then placed on my head. Do you know what!? I could see everything very clearly through those two holes! I could even feel the little pumpkin sway, so I was careful when I moved my head, to make sure that my head-dress didn't fall off. Then, to make me look even more festive, Ma tied a matching orange ribbon near the end of my tail. Satisfied with her workmanship, and with me - her superb model - she proclaimed, "There now, Blackie, now you're all set for Halloween!"

To further add to the upcoming festivities, Ma had carved a huge pumpkin into a jack-o-lantern. But this jack-o-lantern did not have a scary face; it had a mischievous grin! Posing together Ma took a picture of me and jack-o-lantern. Then she removed my costume, telling me that I'd be wearing it again in a few days.

A few days passed. I was again arrayed in my Halloween outfit. Ma explained that jack-o-lantern and I would welcome the children from the area as they came to *trick-or-treat*. As the children arrived we were surprised to see the excellent variety of costumes they wore. But, we almost couldn't congratulate them on how they looked because as soon as they saw me and my jack-o-lantern, they squealed with delight. As Ma handed out the *goodies*, the children thanked her, but they were more interested in me and my costume! I was not allowed to have any of the goodies, especially chocolate, which Ma says can be fatal to cats. You know what? I didn't really care if I missed out on any of the goodies. I was happy just greeting the children. I greatly enjoyed their reactions to me. I felt like a star! Not Felix, not Garfield, not even Cary Grant could hold a candle to me! I felt so very dapper, I didn't even need a top-hat!

When the last of the children had said good-bye, and headed back home with all of Ma's goodies, we sighed. We knew we would remember them in their costumes, and especially how happy they were to see us. We were sure that they would carry, for months to come, good memories of me in my costume and Mr. Jack-o-Lantern's genial grin. As Ma carefully removed the costume from me, so she could pack it away for next year, she commended me on my performance, saying she was *pleased as punch* with me. As I watched Ma pack the costume, I wondered where she would keep it. Then I thought about where I would keep my memories of that night. It's funny, I know there's always enough space in our minds for our best memories, I just wondered where in my mind I was going to keep this one, so I could find it real easy. And, I do recall getting an extra helping of my favorite brew that night. In fact, I can still recall the taste of the catnip on my tongue as a reward for my performance on that special Halloween night. I guess the tongue is as good a place as any to keep a good memory.

'Twas groundless fight where the two cats met,
With frightful hiss howl zoom and high arched back.
Each cat scrambled, rolled, dived in counter-attack.
'Twas fuzzy sight, two furry flights, one saber jet.

16

Fighting Cats

*W*hen outside, I would sometimes follow the well-worn paths in the grass around the house, made by the barn cats. Some of the cats used them systematically in their reconnaissance tours of the house grounds. Following the paths, the barn cats might chance upon a poor bird which, not having calculated a window as such, had crashed into a clear pane, and plummeted fatally to the ground. Occasionally, one of the cats would pause along a path to bask, if it was a sunny day, or to lay in the warmth against the foundation of the house.

I think all our paths are linked somehow. For example, I've often crossed the path of other creatures, too. I've even watched an earthworm on its path, a path I could not follow, nor would I want to if I could. I've seen many earthworms slowly slither across the blacktop driveway, after a spring rain. They very laboriously, and bravely, make a path, going from one little puddle of water to the next, drawing fuel from each as they work their way through a myriad of obstacles such as fallen maple tree blossoms. They are actually racing to get to soft dirt before the wind and sun dry up the puddles of fuel. Sometimes, they do not make it, and are doomed to shrivel up and die, never reaching their destination. They are so vulnerable, and so very brave. They even have to worry about hungry birds, and some of us more roughly curious cats.

One sunny morning, having paused along one of the barn cat paths to bask in the sun, I watched as Ma hung out the wash on the line to dry. From a safe distance, I observed two barn cats eyeing each other with mean intent to maim each other. There was mutual contempt in their eyes as they arched their backs, circling closer and closer together. Although Ma was busy, she, too, was aware that a confrontation was about to take place. Losing no time to contemplate the situation, she hurried into the house for her secret weapon. Before she returned, the two had sprung into action. Sparks literally flew from their eyes; they rolled in furious combat, tufts of fur flying; each cat letting go a series of yowls that would have made a mean dog shudder.

I wondered how either cat could survive such a cruel attack by the other. Just as I was thinking *Ma had better hurry* with her secret weapon, I heard the back door slam and she was on her way. The fighting cats separated for a second and then dove back into each other. At first, I had delighted in watching this fight; but, soon I feared there would be a casualty because of the extreme intensity of the fight. I considered both cats to be my good friends, but good friends or not, I did not want to see either one seriously injured, or worse.

I suppose I should have stepped in, but I was *very familiar* with Ma's secret weapon. I only hoped she could quickly put an end to this fight. She didn't waste any time. She arrived, positioned herself for an accurate shot, which could not have been easy, what with writhing cats and a heavy pail. Hoisting the pail directly over their heads, she released its contents. Bingo! Right on target. With the deluge of water, the cats separated, soaked to the skin, and stared at one another for a moment. Then they looked up at Ma and quickly decided they wanted no more of her. They slunk away to salvage what little pride they had left, neither cat able to claim victory.

As Ma finished hanging up the wash, I settled back down to continue my basking. As I settled down, I noticed that whenever Ma would hang a piece of clothing, like one of her blouses, on the line, the line would vibrate, causing every other piece of clothing to shake, all along the line, even down to other end, where pairs of Pa's long-johns danced in the sunshine. It suddenly occurred to me that we are all linked together like the clothes hanging from Ma's line. Whatever disturbs the line disturbs everything attached to it. The same must be true of all our paths. A disturbance or an obstacle in one path affects all other paths linked to it.

Neither *glorious victory* nor *ignominious defeat* is ever permanent in the animal world, in any world, for that matter. Indeed, since we all are linked together like the clothes hanging from Ma's clothesline, a break at any point in the line destroys the connection and causes all the clothes to fall. So, it seems clear to me, though I am only a cat, that it's much more practical for all of us to cooperate in all things, or else our whole world could collapse. And, speaking of hanging, wasn't it Ben Franklin, at the time of the American Declaration of Independence, who said, "We must all hang together, or most assuredly, we'll all hang separately?" For Franklin, fighting for freedom from tyranny and mistreatment was the only thing ever worth fighting for. He wasn't thinking of us cats when he said it, but we surely are included now. And some cats, as you know, think for themselves; in fact, *most* cats are highly *independent* thinkers! Oh, well. The sun here, on this path, now seems nicer and warmer and much more civil. Come to think of it, the very same sun shines on you, too.

76

Too many cats use genetic progression when they multiply.
Naturally expressing themselves by geometric exponential,
Serenely oblivious to the numbers they are measured by,
They become lost digits in a math of ubiquitous credential.

17

A Summer Campaign

I remember the summer Ma and Pa put on a campaign. It wasn't a political campaign, but a campaign of humane nature. Ma and Pa decided they didn't need any more mouths to feed. So they embarked on a campaign to have every one of the barn cats either spayed or neutered.

One by one, the cats were taken to the Animal Hospital located, very conveniently it seemed to me, just down the road and around our country corner. It was the same hospital where I had my surgery and where I was taken once a year for my annual check-up. My annual check-ups consisted of rabies vaccination, leukemia shot, fecal check for worms, upper respiratory check, etc.

Ma played a very big role in my continued good health. She was always doing things to boost my health, not very big things when taken separately, but very big when added up to the great health I was always in. Things like including dry cat food in my diet to help keep my teeth clean. She bought highly nutritional, nationally advertised brands of both dry and canned cat food. Another thing Ma does for me is brush my hair periodically to keep me well-groomed. In addition, the brushing always gives me a physically pleasant feeling. Because Ma allows me the privilege to run outside, for healthy exercise and sun, I have to be checked and treated occasionally for worms and fleas.

I've thought a lot about this topic, something you might be surprised to find a cat doing, besides sleeping a lot. But, I am in favor of the spaying and neutering of pets, especially dogs. But seriously, when Ma told me the truth and let me hear some rather sad statistics, this was the only conclusion I could come to. Consider this: One unspayed female cat and her mate, and all their offspring, producing 2 litters per year with only 2.8 surviving kittens per litter, can total:

in 1 year........	12 cats
in 2 years.......	67 cats
in 3 years......	367 cats
in 4 years......	2,107 cats
and so on and on....	

Not to mention all those dogs it would take to chase us! Really, these figures are staggering. I have been told that there are now over *118,000,000* dogs and cats in the United States. That's incredible, especially considering how many of them end up abandoned, or worse, each year.

Really, Bo and Fluff and I were so lucky to find someone who would be good to us and care for our welfare. It is true that there are so many others not as fortunate as us. Persons like Ma and Pa, and even poor Old Man and Old Woman, are the exception rather than the rule.

Getting back to the summer campaign: Pa went out and bought a large wire cage from a local pet store. The cage was approximately 3 feet by 3 feet, very suitable for the campaign. Each cat was brought in from the barn and placed in the cage the night before his or her scheduled trip to the hospital. The cage was large enough to accommodate a litter pan, food and water dishes, and still have room enough for a cat to comfortably relax. Most of the cats were quite cooperative, for, they enjoyed the individual attention and pampering they experienced while being caged. This was something they didn't get among the many cats in the barn. Others were a bit apprehensive, but came around with Ma's soothing words and lots of attention. Of course, a little bit of attention in the form of extra special food, like canned tuna, was guaranteed to be soothing.

The routine of the campaign lasted almost three full months. Each cat was caged and fed by a certain hour, then transported to the Vet for a morning surgery. After surgery the cat was brought home and kept quietly caged for three days to recover. I tried, but could not gain close access to the cage to look in on the patients. Ma knew I'd be curious, so she placed the cage very strategically on the corner of the ping-pong table and covered the top and two sides with black plastic. Otherwise, I easily would have been able to see each patient. The only way I could see my friends was from the front of the cage, but only while standing below, on the floor. I couldn't even get a glimpse of the gal cats! Of course, it was wonderful just to know that Bo and Fluff were in my quarters when it came their turn.

Ma and Pa, and most certainly the Vet, knew what they were doing, so everything was kept very orderly and the whole campaign proceeded smoothly. I was not ignored during this long busy period, either. In fact, Ma seemed to show me even more affection and made me feel very special, too. So the days rolled by as twelve of my barn friends, and, of course, Bo and Fluff, made the trip to the Vet and back. They all became healthier and happier cats, for, after the surgery, there was no more vying amongst one-another for supremacy, and no more fierce battles. Instead, a peaceful, if somewhat neutral, at-mosphere reigned in our now calm cat world.

Ma said such fine and sophisticated cats should now be personally recognized and so, as they returned from the Vet, each and every one of them was officially named and given a generous portion of catnip. Of course, each of their names befitted their character and appearance. Most of the cats appreciated seeing their names in the fine and delicate cursive used to exquisitely write their names on a *Registry of Occupants* that Ma put up in the barn, near the door. Ma knew all the cats quite well. After all, she'd been in close contact with each of them at least twice a day at feeding time and occasionally encountering them as she worked around in the yard. She had had no trouble finding suitable names for each of them. Some were friendly, others aloof; there was only one that was a real nuisance. So far as I could see, all of them seemed to be pretty much the same in character before and after their visits to the Vet. Ma wrote all their names down for me on a pretty pink sheet of paper under the heading,

Blackie 'Ice' Berg's Extended Family

Graydash, Creampuff, Mischief,
Whitey, Rusty, Chelsea,
Midnight, Sweetie, Sootie,
Whisper, Delsey,
Bo, Fluff,
Nuisance.

Note: See last page. Please fill it in and become a member of my extended family, too! You can send a photo (or a copy of the page) to the publisher, attention, "Ice" Berg and I will try to answer any question you might have. We all look forward to meeting you and your friends. Thank you very much. Your friend, *Blackie.*

Oh, to be safe as a cat in a comic
Who can speak from inside a balloon.
Who can drive a dog totally ballistic,
Tweaking his nose from inside a cartoon!

18

Enjoying the Comics

$\mathcal{L}$ately, Ma had taken to reading the daily paper in the afternoon while she took a break from her busy day. I would often sit nearby and take a cat nap. One day, I was not particularly inclined to nap. So, I decided to watch Ma closely as she turned each page of the newspaper. Her facial expressions ranged from sad disbelief, to serious, to placid, to pursed smile, as she progressed through the news. Then, as she was almost finished, very near the end of the newspaper, her expression changed very noticeably. Clearly, she had found something in which she could express sheer delight. I edged as close as I could to see what she was looking at. It was the comics! Then she laughed out loud, and her laughing made me laugh, too, but I didn't know why or at what.

I decided I would try to find out what made her so happy when she reached that section of the paper. So, I walked right up to her and looked questioningly into her eyes. Reaching down, stroking my head, she asked, "Blackie, would you like to read the funnies?" I gave her an affirmative *meow*, as I jumped into her lap. Using her

81

finger as a pointer, for she always enjoyed being a teacher, she described the pictures, trying very hard to keep from laughing, as she re-read what had been so funny to her. The lesson was a lot for me to try to comprehend at one time, but after digesting the words in conjunction with the pictures, the humor finally started to shine through.

My first lesson in reading the comics involved *Kit 'N Carlyle* and *Garfield.* I discovered that both of them had a lot in common with me. I had to agree with Ma, they both could be very funny indeed. Imagine that! Me, reading the *funnies*! Ha ha! If you want to know the truth, though, I laughed even harder when I saw Ma laugh at me laughing at her. Funny, how funnies seem to focus in on what's funny. So what's the use of funnies, anyway? I figure there must be a little mirror in every laugh we make, because each laugh seems to reflect more and more laughs. Maybe it would be easier if we all read the newspapers starting with the funnies. It's difficult to wade through all the sad news first. Besides, starting with the funnies might make us laugh, then we'd laugh at each other laughing at each other, laughing so much we'd never even get to the sad news!

Pa wanted to get a photograph of us laughing. But Ma is not as photogenic as I am, so she always refused to have her picture taken. I sometimes wonder if a picture of us laughing would make us laugh. Maybe that's what Ma was really afraid of. Anyway, I did begin to enjoy reading the funnies. Ma would sometimes leave the paper open at the page they were on so I could enjoy them at my leisure.

Ma didn't have much spare time. What little she had, she spent painting. And what was left over, she spent reading. Often, when she was reading something particularly enlightening, she would invite me up on her lap to further my education, er, that is my edu-*cat*-ion. One classic I must say I enjoyed especially was the book of cat poems by T. S. Eliot. It occurs to me that my friend and neighbor, C. H. E. Shire, might want to take a lesson or two from *Old Possum*. Mr. Eliot's poems are very cleverly and uniquely done and Ma would read them aloud and show me the illustrations. Funny, she would read only one poem at a time, saving the rest to be read at intervals, so the enjoyment could be spread out over a longer period of time. I wondered if there was some way we could do that with tuna casseroles and ice-cream cones.

Ma always kept me informed, through the newspaper pictures, of all the cat shows. I've never been allowed to go to one, but Ma said I'd win the first prize ribbon, *hands down*, if I ever did go. I've read that ordinary house cats, like me I suppose, have indeed taken ribbons at some of the fanciest shows. I've often felt that I would be on my very best behavior if Ma ever entered me in a local show. But, after all, what did I need a ribbon for? I know I'm a winner in Ma's heart and that's all that really counts anyway.

I will tell you about a thrill I had the other day. Ma had left a page of the newspaper open on the table, purposely, I suspect. When I took a close look, as I usually did, I saw that two very famous cats were making a local appearance. One was an orange tabby, named *Monster*, who was Data's cat on *Star Trek: The Next Generation*. The other was *Gimmel*, the *Fancy Feast* company cat. Both of those fellows were specimens to be admired. Just seeing their pictures in the paper and reading about them really made my day!

I am, myself, somewhat of a local celebrity. I actually have my own paw prints set in concrete. It wasn't as though I had planned it, exactly. You see, I innocently sauntered across the wet cement, when the floor of my apartment was being repaired. Ma said that now we didn't need to go to California, because we had our own walkway of stars: My footprints, and the stars she saw when she saw them there!

A bowl of milk makes a cat imperial.
But, a floor of milk makes a cat comatose.
Better make some toast, add some cereal.
Or else a cat might overdose on lactose!

19

Spilt Milk

*L*et me tell you about the day Ma came home with her weekly groceries and I *suffered* a special treat. That day, as was my usual custom, I ran to greet her, anxious to see if she'd brought me a special treat, such as my favorite food, fish. She had brought in all the bags except one. Before she returned to the mechanical for it, she set two one-gallon jugs of milk down on the counter. She made the mistake of putting one of the jugs on the counter-saver, which had a slight tilt to it. The jug slid from the tilted counter-saver and come crashing to the floor right next to me. I could have been knocked out. I was dazed, startled, and covered head to toe and tail with milk. My eyes grew as big as saucers at the sight of all that milk! There was enough milk at my feet to last me for weeks!

I jumped to a dry spot under a nearby chair. Peering out from under the chair seat, I saw Ma's face as she returned to the kitchen with the last bag of groceries. She stopped dead in her tracks. She exclaimed, "Oh no!" She gave me an accusing glance. Her expression at me spoke louder than words. I felt really bad. In spite of her consternated look, I remember thinking she might drop the last bag, too; a few cookies would go good with the milk. *When it rains, it pours*, you know. But, the initial shock wore off quickly. There was no place in the kitchen, other than my spot under that chair, dry enough to set the bag down. So, Ma retraced her steps and set the bag of groceries down in the breezeway. Everything had been splashed with milk, all the cupboards, the stove, refrigerator, chair seats, table, and even the walls. Many months later Ma even found a spot or two dried on the ceiling. My recovery was even quicker than Ma's. I started to lap up that milk as fast as I could. No way was I going to *cry over spilt milk*!!

Ma got busy at once. She rolled up her sleeves and *took the bull by the horns*, so to speak. She collected her cleaning supplies and began to clean up the mess. I continued to lap, stopping now and then to rest my tongue. I glanced at Ma as she worked diligently. I noticed that she never stopped to take a break or grab a refreshment. She did, however, glance frequently at me, her eyes shooting darts of accusation. I was lapping as fast as I could. What more could I do? I also observed that my efforts to help made very little impression in cleaning up the floor.

Once again, Ma turned in my direction with that accusing look. I felt so wrongly accused that I actually thought of doing a couple of flip-flops right over the spots she had cleaned. But, that is really not me. Besides, I was too full of milk. I could see, the way Ma was working, that my supply of milk was not going to last as long as I had first thought. So I tried to hurry my lapping. Soon, I couldn't drink another drop. I thought of asking Ma if Bo and Fluff and some of the other cats could come in to help, but she seemed too busy and too perturbed at me to risk adding more cats to the scene.

I was really uncomfortably full. Ma realized that I may have consumed too much milk. She told me, rather harshly, to stand back and stop drinking. "If you drink any more, Blackie, you'll end up getting sick!" She was right. I could have developed a dreadful condition known as lactose intolerance.

So I stood back and watched Ma as she continued to labor to restore the sparkle to her kitchen. Peering down at my fur, I saw that I had plenty of cleaning of my own to do. After an hour or so, Ma had the kitchen back to normal. She then slumped down in a chair and wiped her forehead. I heard her mumble something like, "How could I have been so careless?" Well, when I heard her say that, I knew she was no longer blaming me for the accident, and she had taken full responsibility.

Later, as I busied myself cleaning the milk from my coat, I thought, "I can't ever remember tasting so good!" I realized that I would have to get outside to eat plenty of grass to help me bring up the hair balls that were most certainly going to develop from all my self-grooming. Ma looked down at me as I worked to clean myself up. She laughed and said "No use crying over spilled milk." I chuckled as she opened the kitchen door and let me out. I thought, "Now I know why you should never put all your milk in one container."

Never is down so down, or up so up
That down stays down, or up stays up.
So, ups go down and downs go up!

20

Ups and Downs

*W*e all have our ups and downs. Even Ma. But not all the ups are nearly that up, and not all the downs are nearly that down. I recall one particular downer of Ma's that wasn't nearly so down as some downs are.

I had not been to the barn lately to see brother Bo and sister Fluff, so I thought I'd go out with Ma when she fed all the barn cats. While I cat-talked with Bo and Fluff, Ma spread out food on the linoleum dinner table. Suddenly she lost her balance. She had just finished filling one of the large water pans. Still holding on to the other empty pan, somehow her feet twisted, causing her to slip. She fell backwards and her hip hit the lip of the large water pan, making it flip over into her lap, splashing water all over her. Talk about making a dramatically big splash! The empty pan in her hand struck the concrete floor with such a loud bang that it scared all us cats. We made a mad dash to the safety of the hay bales. Ma could see us all staring back at her.

She struggled to her feet, assessed the damage inflicted on herself, and then looked back at us cats, and shrugged her shoulders. Later she told me she was amazed that she had no broken bones and very few bruises. Perhaps it was because she had fallen onto the large pan of water, which broke her fall and acted somewhat like a waterbed. Or, perhaps it was because the empty pan she held acted like a cushion to absorb most of the force of the impact. The only damage she incurred was a thoroughly soaked dress, which could easily be dried out when she got back to the house. When we all realized that she was not injured, we began to laugh so loud that Ma looked at us sternly saying, "Oh, shush!"

The barn cats slowly returned to their dinner plate and resumed their meal. Nurturing only a hurt pride, Ma filled up both of the water pans, and quietly picked up her utensils. Together, we walked back to the house. I was very careful not to say a word. I don't think Ma ever told Pa about this particular downer. I remember thinking, "sometimes it takes a good fall to remind us we can still get up if we have to."

There's a call, so sweetly soft and mild,
Calms wayward child, tames wildest wild,
Reaches out as far as we are apt to roam.
A Mother's call that always brings us home.

21

When Ma Calls

*M*a was usually soft-spoken and very seldom raised her voice. On occasion, however, she would exercise a very healthy pair of lungs. Usually, Ma would only raise her voice to call me in for a meal or to get me back in to the safety of my quarters if she and Pa were going away for awhile. On good exploring days, I would wander a *fur* piece from home, most likely down by the creek, where chasing rats or frog plopping was usually good.

If I had an extra long chase or a distant exploration, and was really hungry, I'd cover the distance from the creek to the house, upon hearing Ma call, "*Black-i-e-e-e*!" with leaps and bounds in a matter of seconds, hurtling the uneven turf with ease and grace, proud of my sure-footedness. But, if the chase was good and I didn't want to stop, it was not inconceivable of me, on purpose you understand, to pretend that I had not heard her call. At these times, when I didn't respond, Ma's voice took on a frantic intense tone. It was kind of like the sound of a freight train. I knew it meant get in here right now, or you'll know what the cow bumper on a locomotive feels like to a lingering cow. Eventually Ma came to learn to

92

anticipate my possible delay and would call me earlier than when she actually wanted me in. That way, she hardly had to raise her voice. Of course, I could tell when there was no urgency in her voice, so would often wait until I heard her second summons and, on occasion, even her third call.

Ma also soon learned another trick to get me to be more prompt. I could not resist the promise of catnip. That never failed to bring me on the run. I could recognize the exact tone of Ma's call when catnip was on the near end of her voice. Catnip was always good to eat, but I also liked to save some to roll in. Something in its aroma makes me feel good and I get very frisky. So, over the years, we learned each others' tricks, much to our mutual benefit. So, Ma seldom had to raise her voice to the level of a freight train bearing down on me. Believe me, I preferred it that way, and I knew when to *moo-ve* it when I had to.

Every Vet seems to know exactly how a cat is able to purr,
Except the cat itself. But, ask a cat why and it will casually say:
"It's a species-peculiar phenomenon that predictably will occur
Close to a dish of tuna or when I am stroked in my favorite way."

22

Stroking

Ma didn't know it, but I preferred to be let in the house by way of the patio. Coming in this route gave me an opportunity to sneak into the livingroom and rub up against Pa's feet as he sat in his reclining chair. Sometimes he would invite me up on his lap for a session of petting. His large warm hands always seemed to deliver such comforting strokes.

Before going back to my quarters, if the invitation was out, I'd run to Ma and she would rub my ears and scratch my head. Then she would gather me up in her arms. She would place her two hands under my belly. This was an especially comfortable position for me to be carried in, and --- as Ma soon realized --- it was also a position from which it was nearly impossible for me to wiggle free, even if I wanted.

Cats, I think, can be very independent and some-times even moody, I guess. Maybe you could say I am a spirited cat, too. For example, if I was ready to go down the stairs to my quarters for the evening, Ma never had any problems getting me to go. But, if I was in a mood to linger, I sometimes would thrust a paw at her just before she shut the door behind me. I guess you could say that it was important for me to sometimes show a bit of rebellion and to show I didn't like to be entirely controlled. On the other paw, if I was ready and agreeable to go down to my quarters, I'd stop halfway down the cellar steps, look back at Ma and twitch my tail several times in agreeable acknowledgment to her soothing words, "Good boy! Good boy!"

Funny, how we get to know one another when we pay attention to each other. Sometimes, just paying attention is a kind of stroking. And sometimes a little bit of rebellion leads to a little bit of attention. We cats know all this instinctively, you know.

If a woodchuck could chuck wood ...
Then a woodchuck would chuck wood so good ---
He'd have no time to raid the garden for food,
To munch on melons or ruin Ma's good mood!!

23

Garden Bandits

I looked forward to spring. I always felt somewhat cooped-up during the winter. I could hardly wait until Ma got into her old duds and we started to plant the garden together. Of course, I'm probably more of a hindrance than a help. I do knock over row markers. I do roll around in the fine soil where little seeds have been planted. But mostly I'm just underfoot. I really try to help, but there's just so much distraction. I have to blame it on my nature, since my nature seems to want to mostly play around. Ma must certainly value my company, since she always puts up with me and my antics.

This year was no different. While the garden was being planted with beans, carrots, beets, corn, sweet potatoes, etc., *but no melons*, we noticed mother wood-chuck giving lessons to her young on how to harvest, rather *how to eradicate*, Ma's garden. Mother woodchuck stressed to her young the importance of an early harvest. This meant, of course, chewing up anything green. A really good harvesting job involved chewing off all the plants at ground level. I suspect mother woodchuck was an excellent teacher, judging by the damage done to Ma's garden.

Ma liked to work in the garden. But, naturally, she wanted to have something to show for her efforts. She always planted more than she or Pa could use. She hoped there would be enough for everyone. Ma enlisted the help of some carefully groomed scarecrows, setting them to guard duty at strategically located spots around the garden. The scarecrows did a good job. That is they did a good job until two bandit families joined forces against them. The families of *Raccoon Wise* and *Woodchuck Brazen* moved into the garden full strength. They overwhelmed the scarecrows by simply ignoring them. When Ma surveyed the damage, she took down the scarecrows and raised a white flag. That was the end of gardening that year for Ma. Her decision surprised me and also ended my much-looked-forward-to entertainment. After all, I *kind-of* liked to be as helpful as possible with gardening.

It seems to me that the Wise and Brazen bandits ended up stealing themselves out of a good food supply by their insatiable greed. In fact, we all lost out. That's the way it always goes, when one group totally ignores the wants and needs of another group.

Know the cottonmouth in water, the diamondback on prairie,
Each strikes a fatal pose; but, beware the brazen copperhead
As it in forest color goes, it's said to zig & zag in pink or red.
Nor marriage rose nor promise does the golden garter carry.

24

The Snake

*M*y apartment has many amenities. There are two big wash tubs. I can always find enough fresh water in the bottom of one to quench my thirst on occasion, if my regular water bowl is empty. For some reason, the water from a tub seems to taste better to me. There is a furnace, which is really just a gigantic metal box that hums when it runs. It gives off lots of nice warm air when it is cold outside. There is also a deep freezer. I jump on top of it in summer to cool my paws. There's even an old TV, though I rarely like to watch it, unless there's a good cat episode on. And, my windows have curtains. I do have a complaint about curtains. I'd just like to have less of them and more look-out to-see-the-world space.

Various pieces of wearing apparel, mostly work clothes, are always draped around on hooks. The duds add a touch of atmosphere, a kind of casual ambiance, to my apartment. I like to try to identify the curious outdoor smells the clothes give off before they are washed. And there's lots of barn cat food stored in one corner. I've been known to do a pretty good job in getting into the food sacks once they've been opened, especially when I'm real hungry and I've already emptied my own dish. In the process of gaining access, I leave the sack tops in a rather ragged state of disrepair. So, Ma knows I won't be too hungry when she does come to fill my dish. There's always evidence, and the evidence always tells.

Also, there are two water tanks down here. You've already heard about the one that *sprung a leak*, causing a mini-flood. All these amenities have played an interesting role in my life. I could tell you a good story about each of them. If I did, almost all the stories would have a good ending. I think that's in keeping with the more domestic side of my basic nature. You know, we cats always land on our feet, or someone's shoulder as I did when the basement flooded.

For example, let me tell you my story about corralling a crafty coral. One day, while sauntering around my quarters, I passed close to one of the water tanks. It is elevated an inch or so above the concrete floor. I sensed something was moving underneath the tank. Whatever it was, it was moving very, very slowly. Being a very patient fellow, I decided to wait. I crouched in front of the tank, keeping my eye trained on an area beneath. As an experienced hunter, I knew that stealth, in this case absolute stillness on my part, was a great tactical strategy, especially when confronting the unknown.

My patient wait paid off. A dark shiny knob appeared under the bottom rim of the tank. I could not see clearly what it was. I waited for it to come out where I might be able to take a swipe at it, whatever it was. Then it appeared. Right in front of me was a snake! A moving target. As it slithered out from under the tank, I tried to stop it by gingerly dabbing at it with an outstretched paw. I knew Ma would not abide having a snake in my apartment. As it tried to slither past me, I must have dazed it with one of my deltoid power jabs. It probably decided just to stay put right there, rather than risk any more power taps from me. I did not really try to harm the snake, for I thought it was, after all, an innocent living creature just trying to get by. But, I did toy with it a little, just to see if it would try to make a run back to the water tank.

I was glad that Bo and Fluff were not there, for I feared they might have less control of themselves. Finally, I was convinced that the snake would lay still and not try to hide from me or from Ma. Since it was not moving, and seemed even more patient than me, I turned my attention elsewhere.

It was time for me to eat. I knew Ma would soon be coming down to prepare my meal. I decided to play a trick on her. I would not warn her of the snake's presence. Since it lay motionless, out in the middle of the floor in plain sight, she would be sure to see it as soon as she came down. Of all the creatures in this world that Ma loves, or at least peacefully tolerates, snakes and dirt spiders were *very* far down on her list. I looked forward to see her comical shudder when she spotted the snake.

My plan to have a little bit of fun back-fired. It was Pa who came to fill my dish this time! Pa had no reaction at all. He nonchalantly picked up the snake and took it out to the field behind the garden, where he released it. Later, he mentioned to Ma that I had *hypnotized* a young milk snake. Pa said it looked like a coral snake, but the coral, which is poisonous, is found in the southern states, not up north. When Pa asked Ma to keep an eye on the cows to make sure that the snake wasn't taking too much milk, Ma said, "Oh, gosh. That's just an *old wives tale*!" Pa laughed and responded, "Oh, I don't know. There's *a lot of truth* in those old wives' tales." I didn't say anything. But, oh, man. If I'd known a coral was *poisonous* I would have treated that snake a lot more harshly. But, I would have been wrong, and would have ended up harming an innocent young milk snake, not at all what I thought it was. To be sure, here was another argument in support of my live-and-let-live leanings!

The next day, Ma thanked me for flushing out the snake. She praised me for my hunting skill and hoped that I would be just as diligent if there were any more snakes left in my apartment. Obviously, neither of us would call a snake an amenity, since amenities rarely move by themselves! And, talk about a letdown! After all my planning to get a good rouse from Ma, all I get is a pat on the head and a keep-it-up pep-talk! Oh, well. I guess it's true: The best laid plans of men *and cats* (and snakes) go oft' amiss!

If you wish, on eve, alone upon a lakeside ledge,
Makes no difference what you wish or pledge.
When setting sun tosses a golden anchor out to you,
Then you may be sure your wish has come true!

25

Our Wish Lists

Ma was always buying me surprises. One day, she bought me my own scratching pad. This gift came partly in response to the scratch marks I had placed strategically on the casing of the kitchen door. The surface of the new pad served to keep my claws in good shape. I enjoyed using it regularly, especially when Ma would lace it with catnip. But, soon the scratching pad was worn-out and I resumed my affronts to the kitchen door.

The damage had already long been done, so I was not reprimanded when I again began to scratch my claws on the door base. Sometimes, I would scratch at the door in order to alert Ma or Pa that I wanted to go out. Ma promised to bring me a small log to do my claw sharpening on, but there had to be another way figured out for me to be able to signal them that I wanted to go out. I thought about asking Pa to build some sort of lever that, when I pushed down on it, would uncover a "Cat Wants Out," sign on the other side of the door. Then, when either Ma or Pa let me out, the "Wants," part of the sign could be covered, leaving just the words, "Cat Out." This would be a good way for

Ma and Pa to also know that I was, in fact, out when I was out. I will ask Pa to patent this idea, too.

There were days that I would get bored and very lonesome, especially in the winter, when I couldn't go outside because of the cold. I would think back and yearn for the affection that I had received from Mom-Mew in my early days. So, with this memory recalled, I could be quite demanding that Ma keep me company. But, she had so many other commitments that I had to spend some time alone. Once, just so I would have company, she had offered to bring one other cat in from the barn, but, I quickly declined her offer as I did not want to share her affection or, even worse, risk the disappointing return of a cat to the barn after he or she had had a taste of life in the white house. Suddenly, I had a marvelous idea. I would ask if Bo and Fluff could join me, for it would be wonderful to have them with me again. They would understand if they had to return to the barn later. But, Ma had insisted that there be only one cat, and so --- not wanting to separate the two of them --- I had to discard this idea, though I thought it would be a most excellent arrangement.

Sometimes, with my best interest at heart, she would leave the TV or radio on, when she temporarily left the basement. The TV shows were of no interest to me, for truthfully, I didn't know what those *soaps* were all about. Frankly they were too mushy for me! Oh, they did break the silence, but they were no substitute for a romp with Ma. I loved playing hide and seek, or catch the cob. Ma would trail a corncob on a rope for me to try and catch, as she walked rapidly around the basement. I suspected that this was a good way for her to get some extra exercise in the hope of losing a winter pound or two, also.

One day Ma presented me with a beautiful pheasant feather. It became a favorite toy of mine. It soon frayed, however. I was too rough on it. I need to invent a feather that doesn't lose its feathers! It was always a struggle to keep from putting on weight during the winter months. Ma got a prescription from the Vet to help me with my food elimination and keep me from getting fat and lethargic and maybe sick. Ma would slip the pill into my food. I always knew it was there, but never complained, for Ma always seemed to know best, and I trusted her judgment in these matters. In the short run, it did make more work for her, though, because she had to empty my litter box more frequently. In the long run it probably saved us both from a lot of extra work and grief.

There is one exercise that I don't think anyone could ever make a machine for. I call it the *brace and rub* roll. When Ma was doing dishes, she would kick off her shoes and invite me to brace my feet against the lower cupboard. Then she would rub my back and my sides with her stocking feet. Ma's legs must have ached after doing this little exercise for as long as I liked having it done! She always had to hold her feet in such an awkward position, but oh how I *loved* that rubdown.

Ma had promised several times to get me a privacy screen for my bathroom. Instead, she put up a sign which reads: "Blackie's Commode." Just how did she think that sign would solve my privacy problem? Her thinking was not very clear on this point. But, I love her anyway.

Another lovely promise that needs to be fulfilled somehow is the oat patch that Ma wanted to grow in my apartment. Ma figured she could bring in some oat seed from the granary and plant it in a flatbed so it would grow during the winter. That way I'd have a constant source of grass to help bring up my hairballs. Ma still goes outside and digs under the snow to bring in some faded grass for me. It is a poor substitute for my summer chew, but it usually does the job.

Occasionally I was allowed to go upstairs to the second floor of the house. There I could peer out at the birds as they hung out in a nearby pear tree. Although the birds were beyond my reach, it was stimulating to me just to see them there. Of course, the best place to bird watch was below the bird feeders. It had to be something primitive in my nature that could make me enjoy sitting there for hours. In the winter I stuck out against the snow like a red cloak on field of blue, or as Ma would say, "Like a splash of vermilion in a cerulean sky." Since the birds always knew exactly where I was, I seldom was successful in scaring them away or getting close enough to one for a great chase and leap. It might be possible to place a bird feeder close to the ground. But then the squirrels would have a ball. Squirrels are no fun to chase because they always dash off into the nearest tree at the merest sight of someone who might want to hassle them a bit. I just wish there were camouflage lessons for uncamouflaged cats.

On my way to the second floor, I would pass four characters on the stairway. They were, in ascending order: two bears, a dog, and a clown. They paid me no heed as I passed by. I knew they were inanimate, so they didn't intimidate me at all. The clown had a silly grin on his face, as if to imply he knew something that I didn't. The other characters had passive expressions. Ma must have placed them there to add color and character to the stairway. I could see no other use for them at all, especially as they couldn't even wink at me. I wish they were alive; what fun we'd have running up and down the steps and chasing each other around. Ma was perfectly content with things as they were. To her eyes, they did their jobs quietly and without bother; and they successfully decorated and guarded the steps. Still, I wondered why they were not camouflaged.

One day Ma and I watched woodchucks as they prepared a home for winter hibernation. Some people call these animals groundhogs. On February 22 one of them, probably a very wise, very rare and very lovable one, is supposed to be able to predict whether or not there will be six more weeks of winter, based on seeing or not seeing his shadow. Ma and I were surprised to see the woodchucks so busy so late in the fall season. They seemed to work with a frenzy as though they knew winter was near. Despite their short legs they moved very fast over the ground, making many trips, carrying bedding of hay or straw in their mouths, plying back and forth between the barn and their intended winter home. The weather had not yet turned inclement. But, we could see the urgency in their industry. Their instinct proved surprisingly accurate, for the very next day, a considerable amount of snow fell, sealing them snugly in their burrow, where they would remain until spring. Maybe we should have a groundhog day *before* winter, so that the rare and lovable fellow could predict the first snow-fall.

Well, you know we could go on and on with this rather miscellaneous wish list. That's the nature of a wish list. But, Ma has told me that to wish only for myself is very selfish. She says that she always makes one wish that is sure to come true. I will tell you her secret. One of Ma's wishes is that one of *my* wishes comes true. Then, you see, when one of my wishes comes true, one of her wishes comes true, too! Now, I wish that one of her wishes comes true, especially her wish that one of *my* wishes comes true! Oh, oh. I think there is something wrong with this wish. Not only is it selfish, it is as enigmatically unproductive as it is self recursive. What is this cat saying!? Well, maybe that's why we should keep our wishes secret. Anyway, I wish one of *your* wishes comes true! Holy cow! What a great wish! Please let me know when it comes true!

Before the walls of apathy knock you upon your knees,
Lock you in a blameless land where gone your liberties,
Awake! Now fight to save the precious right of all the free
To chose: Should shackles be your last and only dignity?

26

Flight to Freedom

$\mathcal{S}$aturday. So far it had been an uneventful day for me. Ma decided I better stay inside this morning. She was going shopping and the weather looked threatening. She knew how lightening and thunder could frighten any animal out of its wits. So she wanted me to have access to my sanctuary, an untouchable spot of absolute serenity beneath the old TV cabinet. There had been quite a few thunderstorms recently. There was no dust under that old TV. I could attest to that.

Pa was lately handicapped in getting around and Ma didn't want to leave him with the responsibility to try and run me down if I needed to be brought in. She also knew that I would probably sneak upstairs when Pa wasn't looking and get into all sorts of mischief. After all, I did enjoy myself in Ma's old storage room which was crammed wall to wall with this and that and the other thing!

So, here I was, safe and sound in my apartment, but bored! Ma, always wanting to make me happy, had left some catnip. I decided to eat some. It always perked me up and put me in a frisky mood. Boy, did it ever. I decided to get my exercise for the day. I raced lickety-split from the far end of the basement to the other end, jumping up and landing on my much-used ledge. The ledge was fastened to the wood panel of the back door just below the window sill line. I came to a stop in my leap just inches short of the door window pane. I had mastered this jump so I never bashed my nose into the window or otherwise injured myself.

I ran this race and jump several times. It was no fun doing it without an audience. Ma always got a kick out of seeing me do my run and jump, and I enjoyed showing off. Soon, the *storm* hit the area full force. The basement grew very dark except for the light cast intermittently by lightning flashes. I had an eerie feeling that something ominous was about to happen. I headed for the safe spot beneath the old TV. As I peered out, I imagined that lightning had struck very close-by, maybe even hitting our house!

The storm was fierce, but it didn't last very long. It soon abated and everything grew very quiet. I decided to stay under cover for a while, and just to play it safe, crawled under a table and soon fell sound asleep. When I woke up, at first the silence puzzled me. Then I remembered, the storm had passed before I went to sleep. It was reassuring to stretch myself fully awake in the peace and quiet which seemed to pervade the house. Then I heard it. *It* wasn't quiet at all. I heard a strange fluttering noise. I looked around. I couldn't see a thing. Perhaps I was only hearing things. Of course, I was hearing something, but what? Was someone playing magic here? It was frustrating. I couldn't find the source of the noise, let alone find out what was making it.

The mysterious unseen noise kept me occupied until Ma arrived home. While she put away the groceries, I could hear her talking to Pa about her day. Pa was unusually talkative. He was probably telling Ma about how close the storm had come to our house. The kitchen door was slightly ajar. I stood at the opening to listen. I heard Pa mention something about hearing a strange fluttering noise. They agreed it had to be a bird that somehow had gotten trapped somewhere in the walls or vents.

They opened the covers on the cold air vents, since that seemed to be where the fluttering sounds were coming from. But no bird flew out. Then the sound shifted to another area of the wall partition. It was evident that the bird could move about fairly easily. I just got more frustrated. I'm sure Ma and Pa did, too. Everybody had to get resigned to the fact that nothing more could be done for this unfortunate bird. We all resumed our normal activities for the balance of the day.

I awoke Sunday morning to a loud crash. Dazed and not fully awake, I was conscious of a batch of feathers flying by so close to my nose that some of the down stuck to my face and made me sneeze. That's when I first learned that I was allergic to feather down. Add that to the tulip pollen. Now alert, I knew that it was a bird that had buzzed my face! Better a bird than a bat, I thought. The bird must have come out of the hot air pipe. That pipe was the only opening in my apartment. The loud crash that had awakened me was a small bottle that had crashed to the floor. It had been dislodged from the shelf near the open pipe. The bird had flown right into it when it emerged from its confinement.

I was suddenly exhilarated. The chase, and I do mean *the chase*, was on! What strategy should I use to catch that bird? I recall wishing I had wings and could fly. Imagine what that bird was wishing. As I dashed about after the bird as it flew frantically back and forth, I stumbled into a vase filled with flowers, and tipped it over.

Last night Ma had arranged a bouquet of flowers to take to church this morning. Naturally, it had became an innocent target. Water spilled out onto a stack of newspapers Ma was saving for the Boy Scouts. I didn't stop to reflect over this accident, or to consider what reaction Ma might have. I stayed in hot pursuit of this flying ace with its seemingly magical maneuverability. I couldn't help wondering, though, why there were suddenly so many obstacles in my way.

Ma saved most everything. She operated under the assumption that everything could be useful in the future. It's tough for a cat, especially a cat like me, to admit this, but my Ma is a packrat! Ma had even saved a vast quantity of inner tubes from toilet tissue and paper towels. She had them all neatly stacked in a pyramid near one of the far walls of the basement. You guessed it. The bird made a perfect circular loop right over the pyramid and I ran right into the middle of it! I knew they were there, I had seen the pile growing for months. Now, instead of a pile, there was me, doing my best imitation of a log rolling contestant on a river of paper tubes. If rollerderby and rollerblading ever goes professional, I'm destined for stardom, believe me.

Ma opened up the kitchen door to see what all the commotion was about. Just then the bird did a 180 degree turn in front of her face. She literally came flying down the steps with Pa right behind, doing a hitch and pull that almost made him airborne, too. "It's a starling," Ma shouted. "It's a bird," I yelled. "It's a damned shame," Pa moaned. I think Pa was mad that he couldn't fly like the rest of us at that moment. "Leave it to a starling to be where it shouldn't be," Ma laughed.

From past experience, Ma knew exactly what to do. Make the cellar as dark as possible. Open the back door so the bird can see the light. It will fly to the light. This was done, but the poor bird, still confused, had taken refuge among a maze of water pipes and couldn't see the light. In the meantime, Sootie, Midnight, Rusty, Delsy, and Bo, evidently having the best appetites, and wondering where Ma was with their breakfasts, had come sauntering to the house. Seeing the open door, and naturally curious, they just walked right in. As soon as they saw what was going on, they jumped into the hunt, thus adding to the melee! Each cat was sure it would capture that bird.

Well, even I felt sorry for Mr. Jet-ace Starling. Can you imagine that? A cat feeling sorry for a bird? Seeing cats dashing this way and that, all trying to grab him; the poor starling probably wished he was back in the wall. In another frantic attempt to escape the on-coming felines, momentarily fatigued, certainly dazed, he fell to the floor, the wind no longer beneath his wings. Brother Bo was nearest to the fallen bird; but, as he rushed toward him, I made a valiant dash, managing to get in the way. We collided, giving the bird the needed time to recover and move to safer height. Bo and I, just slightly dazed, moved off in continued pursuit, not taking the time to even exchange a "hi," or even an "excuse me."

Mr. Starling had reached a place halfway distant to the back door. Ma quickly picked up a broom and used it to guide the bird closer to the door where it could see the light. She was successful! The starling flew straight as an arrow out the open door into the sunlight and into freedom.

The strange mystery of the fluttering sound had been solved. It remained a mystery, however, as to how the bird got into the wall partition and managed to come out the heating pipe. My apartment looked like a battle zone. Come tomorrow, Monday, instead of doing her wash, Ma would work on cleaning up the cellar, for she was not one to have a mess around for very long.

Midnight, Rusty, Delsey, Bo, and Sootie were rounded up and thanked for their help. Of course, Ma

118

didn't want any of us to be successful. She had held her breath hoping that we would not catch that bird, for all she wanted was to give it its freedom. Actually, we cats all agreed that we were happy to see the bird achieve its freedom, too. Walking back in a group with Ma in the middle, they returned to the barn for their delayed breakfast. Ma pondered, as she tried to hurry them all along, if she would have time to redo the bouquet for that Sunday's church service.

In all my 9 lives, I will never have another weekend quite like that one. I wrote it all down for Aunt Vivian and my good friend, Marian. I wonder if they'll believe these traumatic events. I'm sure the mailman has been wondering about the letters he delivers to them, since they all bear a corner return address with my name, "Ice" Berg, and Ma and Pa's address, accompanied by my paw prints!

To those who are ill to others,
Be they sisters, be they brothers.
Know: All mistreatment we oppose
That to friends and that to foes.

27

A Dream Come True

$\mathcal{I}$t had been an unusually busy day for me. To top it off, it became a very depressing day, as well. My depression was the result of listening that evening to Ma as she read aloud an account in the newspaper of an abused and then abandoned cat. Thankfully, the cruel person responsible for this brutality was apprehended and brought to justice. The account saddened me, for it brought back memories of when Bo, Fluff, and I were abandoned. It also brought back renewed feelings of loss in the mysterious disappearance of our beloved Mom-Mew.

Also, just a few days ago, a new cat had arrived out at the Berg barn. Its grim tale of mistreatment at the hands of its previous owners was all too evident in his appearance. Disturbed by these thoughts, I fell into a fitful sleep. My subconscious mind remained awake and active. It conjured up for me a most eventful dream. In my dream I was to round up all the barn cats and march en masse to the house where the new barn cat had been so mistreated. My dream was amazingly still vivid in my mind when I awoke the next morning. Right then I resolved to make my dream a reality!

Now, thoroughly enthused, I would act as spokes-cat and set about to contact all the barn cats to get their reaction to my mission, and hopefully enlist them in this cause. I knew Bo, Fluff, and Midnight would endorse my plan. They all knew, as did I, the anxiety connected with abandonment. They also knew the dire results of mis-treatment and I was sure they would want to help educate the public in the hope such practices could be eliminated.

I was only able to find and talk to Graydash, Rusty, Chelsea, Mischief, Nuisance, and Delsey. They all agreed to participate. The rest I would have to contact tomorrow, for they could not be reached in time today. The next morning I talked to Creampuff, Whisper, Sootie, Sweetie, and Whitey. The word was already out, and they immediately agreed to participate. Even Newcat, said he would join us if he felt well and strong enough. Eventually all the cats agreed to the plan. I was surprised, for many of the cats were born and raised right here on the farm. I didn't expect them to be concerned, since they had never experienced such adversities in their lifetimes. So, I was really overjoyed to have 100% of the cats agree to participate.

The plan was carefully explained to everybody. We would lose no time. *We would march tonight!* Everyone, including Newcat, showed up at the appointed time. We had to go a considerable distance. When I gave the signal to march, the entourage moved forward. Some were abreast of each other, as were I, Bo, and Fluff. Others followed in a line, as if to draw confidence from the one ahead of them. It was quite a journey and it took many, many steps. Everyone remained enthused in the mission, for there was no complaining along the way. Of course, we kept a close watch for stray dogs. We did, however, stop once so that Newcat, who still was weak, could rest a little to enable him to continue on with us. We were glad he was making the effort, for he was our symbol as well as our evidence - our show and tell.

My mind was at work as we marched along. I thought if we were successful tonight, I would tell Ma what we did, so that perhaps she could have it put in the newspaper, to give other cats, who had been mistreated, the idea to do something similar to help their cause.

Finally, we arrived at our destination - the house where the culprits lived. Lights were still on in the house. This was good, for it very likely indicated that someone was home, and we had not made our long trip for nothing.

Following instructions laid out in our plans, we positioned ourselves strategically in front of the house. It was a clear night. The moon was big and bright and it twinkled through the tree tops. As if in acquiescence to our venture, the tree tops swayed in the gentle warm breeze. When we all were positioned properly, I gave the signal. The most loud, awful, shrill, thunderous moaning and howling you ever heard, the most beautiful sounds we ever made, shook the tree tops and threatened to wake up the dead. Neighbors stuck their heads out their front doors and windows holding their ears. The two occupants of the house appeared on the porch. They began to rant and rave at us, trying to shut us up. The harder they tried the louder we roared. The man went back into the house and came out with a shotgun. He waved it, threatening to shoot at us. We roared even louder. The neighbors called the police. Determined to make our case on behalf of Newcat, we kept up our roar.

When the police arrived a few minutes later, we formed a solid wall of cats and moved in as close to the house as we could. We could see the panic, and the guilt in the two people's eyes. We continued to hiss and to howl. Two policeman walked up on the porch. As they began to speak to the man and the woman, Newcat moved slowly out from in front of our group. He had somehow found the strength to climb up those steps. There he stood defiantly pointing to the man and woman, who had covered their faces with their hands when they saw Newcat.

One of the police officers then turned to all of us and held up his hand, then made a motion to his mouth. We all understood him to be politely asking us to quiet down, so we could hear what they had to say. The man and woman had confessed to the police that they had owned Newcat and had mistreated him and then abandoned him. Both policemen spoke quietly to the man and woman and then nodded in our direction. Then the man admitted to us all, what he had done. And then the woman admitted to us all, what she had done. Then they said to us all and directly to Newcat: "We are sorry for what we did. We will never do such things again." Newcat, hearing this, stood up a little more erect. We all cheered Newcat, as we turned and started to march away. Then did we get a surprise. There was *Chew-Chow* and about thirty of his friends! He just smiled at us, then waved a big mitt at his troops and they all turned around and started to march away from the house. Chew-Chow! He had joined us on our march! What a sight we all must have been as we left the scene in a quiet and orderly fashion. Even Newcat, now with renewed strength, was able to keep up with the rest of us as we returned to the Berg Barn.

Needless to say, I was very proud of all of my friends, and proud of my role in this mission. Rejoicing that my dream had come true, I resolved to speak with Ma in the morning with the hope that our successful mission could be publicized for the benefit of all mistreated felines, and, oh well, *canines*, too.

Fresh strawberries, raspberries, blackberries, all.
Never was the bramble, never was the brier,
So wicked in the field or so thick on the mall,
Could keep us from pickin' for a ripe berry pie.

28

Gone Blackberrying

*M*a must have heard it through the grapevine that the blackberries were ripe. It was a very warm late-summer afternoon. I sat resting on my backdoor ledge. I was frankly bored. There was absolutely nothing moving outside. There weren't even any birds resting in the pear tree to watch.

Suddenly, I heard a mechanical door slam. I wondered who it was. I jumped down from the ledge and proceeded up the cellar stairs. I sat at the closed kitchen door with one ear against the door-bottom, so I could hear.

I heard a conversation, mixed with repeated peals of laughter. I knew it was Aunt Vivian! There seemed to be a lot of commotion in the kitchen. Just then the sliding door opened. I saw then what all the commotion and laughter had been about. I turned and scampered back down the steps. Aunt Vivian came traipsing down carrying two baskets, and Ma followed closely behind her.

It seemed almost every time Ma and her sister, my Aunt Vivian, got together, whatever they said or saw was infectious to them both and sent them into gales of laughter. Could senility be setting in? Aunt Vivian had on

127

a ridiculous outfit. I would rarely comment on wearing apparel, but my dear aunt had gone too far this time. She wore boots which came up to her knees, and she had on a pair of slacks that were way too small, seeing as how she had gained a fair amount of weight during the summer. She also wore a colorful, wildly designed shirt which hung loosely over the top of her slacks. To top it all off, her head looked somewhat tilted beneath a big wide-brimmed straw hat. She looked like an older version of one of Huck Finn's gang. I thought, "Aunt Vivian, get real! It's too summer hot out there today!"

Aunt Vivian had brought me a catnip toy. That was something I would never sneeze at, let alone laugh at. After the usual cordialities were completed, Ma started to dress up, too. She soon looked like a twin to Aunt Vivian, if that were possible, since Ma was a lot thinner. I almost laughed out loud at the two of them. Then I heard Ma say to Aunt Vivian she had heard that the blackberries were good and thick this year.

So *that* was what the Huck Finn imitations were all about. Then Ma took a handful of newspapers and wrapped them around Aunt Vivian's arms. She then secured the newspapers with rubberbands. Aunt Vivian then did the same to Ma's arms. How very strange these women were acting!

They gathered up their baskets and headed for the door. Ma looked back at me and said, "We'll be back after awhile." What! I wasn't invited? I objected as strenuously as I could, "Meow-ow-ow!" Ma explained that it was too far for me to walk on such a hot day. Oh, come on! Why, I wondered, are you both so bundled up if it's that hot out? Ma said she'd explain later, as she opened the door. She and Aunt Vivian were obviously anxious to be on their way.

I had no intention of missing out on something I was sure was going to be lots of fun. So I bolted out through the open door. There was nothing either of them could do to stop me, as bundled up as they were, and lugging baskets beside. They tried to coax me back into the house, even trying to entice me with some catnip. But it didn't work. I was bound and determined that I was going with them. I wanted to meet Huck, too! Finally, Ma agreed to let me tag along. I don't think she really had any choice in the matter.

As we walked through the yard toward the creek, I spotted Graydash. Apparently, Graydash thought Ma was bringing a special treat for the cats in the barn. Anticipating her share, she dashed along in front of us, her tail curled along her back. Our route suddenly turned toward the creek and the lane beyond, where the berry bushes grew. With this change in direction, Graydash realized we weren't heading to the barn after all. Her tail then drooped noticeably. She followed us for a short distance, then headed dejectedly back to the barn. I waved at her to follow us, but she just shook a rather limp paw as a good-bye to me.

We arrived at the creek. I paused at the bridge to look down at the cool wet surface twinkling up at me in the sunlight. I realized I was terribly thirsty. The water in the creek seemed to be inviting me to drink as it meandered along, caressing the marsh grass along the banks. The water level was unusually high for this time of year because we had a heavy rainfall a few days ago. I thought about dashing down to the water for a drink, but then I remembered how I'd almost drowned in that water not long ago. So I scampered ahead to catch up with Ma and Aunt Vivian.

We came to the blackberry patch. Ma and Aunt Vivian got very excited about how many big luscious blackberries were there, waiting to be picked. The grass was tall and dry. It whipped across my hot face as I followed the berrypickers down the lane. They stopped here and there along the way to gradually fill their baskets. Adding to my general discomfort was the presence of hundreds of grasshoppers. Some of them literally jumped into my face. One even flew into my mouth! I was by then extremely hot and thirsty, and I accidentally chomped down on that grasshopper. One would think it might be nice and juicy. Ugh! It was dry and tasted like a piece of straw! I almost didn't even have enough saliva to spit it out. And, it would have been fatal to swallow. I was so hopping mad!

When we reached the end of the lane, I sighed a breath of relief. But, instead of turning around to go back home, the *Huckleberryers* turned down a path into an adjoining lot and followed along a fence which marked the boundary of a twelve acre field! Talk about taxing one's energy! I was so hot and thirsty that I thought I was getting a bit delirious. I started to repeat my name over and over, thinking it would cool me down a little. "Ice Berg. Ice...Ice...Ice Berg. Ice...Ice...!" But, that only made me hotter and thirstier. So much for visualization! *I see*, I-ce not.

The dry grass continued to whip my face as I struggled to keep up with the pickers. Didn't anyone realize it took me at least ten steps, multiplied by four, to equal one of their steps? At one patch, I saw the canes were weighted down to the ground, heavy with fruit. I decided to try and quench my thirst by eating a few of the ripe berries. But the briers were reluctant to release their fruit to me. As I tugged I was promptly caught on the thigh by all the briars. As I tried to jerk myself clear, a cane full of briers latched onto me on the other side. I was gripped so tightly, I felt painfully like a helpless captive. What a blow this was to my masculinity! To think, I couldn't cope with a few *twigs*.

It occurred to me that I should have heeded Ma's directive to stay home, after all.

Ma heard me moan and, seeing my predicament, hurried to my rescue. I then understood why Ma and Aunt Vivian had wrapped their arms. These brambles could be downright vicious! I wondered why I wasn't dressed right for blackberrying. I should have had on a straw hat, bootie pads for my feet and an umbrella to provide shade! I couldn't blame Ma; she had warned me, all right. And she had no chance to prepare me properly. Then I felt somewhat guilty, as I noted how she had to keep a close watch on me to make sure I didn't get all tangled up again, or drop from sun-stroke.

Our trek continued along the fence row. I found a clump of tall grass that afforded me some shade. I lay down and dozed. I dozed to the point of taking a long drink from the laundry tub in my quarters back home. In my doze-dream I thanked Ma for making sure that she kept the tub so clean by swirling fresh cold water round and round in it, letting it drain out anything soapy. That water always tastes so good! When I awoke, there was Ma standing over me, "Come on, Blackie, we're going home now."

We were making good time heading back home when once again Ma and Aunt Vivian stopped. They simply could not resist picking a few more of those danged berries. Ma took off her hat to let the hot breeze blow through her damp hair. She set it down carefully, and I thought very strategically, near a full basket of berries. I didn't need an invitation. I crawled into the shady nook between the basket and the hat.

Then I began to wonder if Ma had purposely sacrificed her own comfort. Had she removed her hat in order to provide me a brief respite from the sun? I shook my head. Talk about my masculinity? As I lay, thankful for this small extension of heaven's space, I saw a tortoise lumber by. He hesitated in his gait, as if to ask, "Why hurry?" Easy for him to say. He carried his shade with him. He was headed toward the creek. It is amazing the superb instincts that God has given all his creatures. How else did this tortoise know which way the creek was from here?

I watched a caterpillar crawl along a twig. Where was *he* going? He *had* to be going somewhere. Somewhere was right, but believe me, there's a lot of *somewhere* out here! When I thought of the distance I had already traveled today, I could only imagine how long it would take this tiny creature to travel as far. Some of God's creatures move very fast, some move slow. In total, I guess, everything is balanced. Had the sun gotten to me? Why was I suddenly so philosophic?

After I had enjoyed this short respite, Ma came back and picked up her hat and basket and we hit the road again. As we all headed off down the road, er *lane*, I wondered why blackberries were black and why strawberries were red. The sun disappeared behind a blanket of clouds. We heard a rumble of thunder in the distance, so it was good we were nearing home at last.

Giant grasshoppers kept jumping in every direction in front us as we neared home. The way they hopped and bounced made me think of the time Ma popped corn without a lid on the kettle. The corn had started popping and she couldn't find the lid in time. Before we knew it, corn was flying all around the kitchen. All I had to do was open my mouth for instant snacks. I like popcorn just as much as my barn friends like melon rinds and sweetpotato skins. And, buttered popcorn was a delicacy to me. But popcorn and grasshoppers? I think the heat was beginning to make my brain sizzle and pop.

When we got back to the house, as soon as Ma opened the door, I bounded in, ran down to my quarters, and made a beeline for the laundry tub. Man, was that the best drink of water I had ever had! Finally, my thirst satisfied, I lay down on my bed, like a ton of bricks. I tell you, I was totally, and I mean totally, exhausted. Before I fell into a deep sleep, I felt something stuck between my teeth. At first I thought it was a grasshopper leg! Had another one of them jumped into my mouth while I was near to passing out with sunstroke? But, thankfully, it was just a briar twig. Oh, well. It would just have to stay stuck right there until I woke up --- in a week or two.

Ma and Aunt Vivian's efforts were rewarded with full containers of berries, very luscious berries. I thought about Pa. He hadn't gone picking, but he soon would be enjoying a very delicious piece of blackberry pie. I, who had endured the heat and agony, was rewarded with utter fatigue, irrational thirst, and a body full of briar scratches! Sometimes, life is just not fair. Never again would I be so insistent in making a trip Ma advised against. OK, I admit it: Ma *always* knows best, most of the time!

With the kitten in the thicket low
The frog will let the cricket go.
With the tadpole at the spigot low
The cat will let the frog go.
The kitten and the cricket never know,
As off they go, to play leap-frog.

29

The Walking Feather,
The Cricket Caper
& The All Night Scare

*I*t was a beautiful fall evening and I decided to stay out a while longer. Ma's first and second calls had already been ignored by me. Winter with its cold weather would soon be here. I didn't look forward to being cooped up for the duration of the cold weather, so I wanted to take advantage of what might prove to be one of the last remaining nice evenings.

I had made acquaintance with a trusting fellow who made a chirping noise by rubbing parts of his forewings together. He looked very large to me when I first saw him, and it seemed he had a habit similar to mine. I always purred when I was happy and content. I had been drawn to this fellow by his chirping. We played a game of pounce and jump. I would pounce at him, then touch him with one of my outstretched paws, and he would jump away. It was great fun. I respected his energy and appreciated the rhythmic sound of his chirps. I tried not to hurt him, his frail body seemed constructed for just one thing, jumping just out of my reach. Although he was one of the larger members of the cricket species, he was really very tiny compared to me.

I always leaped, it was really a miniature pounce, right behind him and part of the fun was timing my leaps so we both would be up in the air at the same time. He often landed before me, but he never leaped away until I landed just behind him and tapped him again. Talk about having 100% confidence in a fellow creature! We had not been engaged in this game of tag for long when I spotted a frog. The frog was crouched in a clump of grass which camouflaged him quite effectively. His eyes were half-closed, in a sly pretense of sleep. I knew the frog was well aware of my friend, the cricket, who must have looked like a great mid-night snack. With a flick of his tongue, that frog could render my cricket friend non-existent. Quick action on my part was necessary to save my friend.

I calculated that two jumps and two pounces would land Mr. Cricket on the tip of Mr. Frog's sticky tongue. This was a tragedy to be averted at all costs. I decided to play leap-frog! I took one giant leap for crickethood. I landed squarely on top of Mr. Frog. He was very nearly squashed. In fact, Mr. Frog could very easily have become Mr. Croak. My little cricket friend was literally saved from the jaws of death. Mr. Frog, though somewhat flattened, was unhurt. He squirmed beneath me in an effort to escape. By squirming so much, he tickled my stomach. I raised myself just enough to let him get away and to give me room to scratch my belly. I watched Mr. Frog hop in a series of beautiful leaps, one right after the other, toward the creek.

Mr. Cricket saw what had happened. He was so thankful, he agreed to a special series of pounce and bounce before we both called it a night. The moon was just coming up. To me, it looked like a huge wheel of yellow cheese. You know how I like cheese, too. The moon peeked above the horizon. It seemed to smile as it rose above the barn roof. And, though it seemed to get smaller as it crept higher in the sky, it cast an ever brighter light, until it shone, round orange and beautiful in full glory, over the farm yard. Filled with the happiness of beauty, I was tempted to raise my head toward this bright beacon and "meow" loudly, much like a dog might howl at the moon. But, bearing in mind who I was, I suppressed this most unnatural desire.

It was getting very late. I wandered closer to the patio door, hoping to hear Ma's next call to come in. But her call never sounded again. All evening I had purposely stayed close to the house so that I would be sure not to miss Ma's third and final call. Crossing the stone walk at the back of the house, my eyes caught a slight movement. The air was still. Not a leaf stirred. Yet, there it was: I saw a small feather move. I watched as it slid slowly and myster-iously along the stone walkway. I've heard of *feathers flying*, but never feathers walking down the sidewalk!

Curiosity killed the cat, they say. I had to find out what was going on here. What harm could there be in a little feather, even in a strange little walking feather? I stood over the feather as it moved. I tilted my head to one side, then to the other. What was going on here? I gently, very gently, extended my paw. As I did so, the feather tipped over. Then I saw what was making it move. Laying on their sides, still firmly gripping the feather above their heads, were three little ants in a row. They looked up at me. Their antennas were shaking like the membranes inside a loud speaker blaring out a shake, rattle, and roll rock song. These three ants, combined, were not as large as one wing of my friend, Mr. Cricket. How could they possibly be moving that feather? I know, you want to say,

"*Easy*, because it was light as a feather!" But, think of it. That feather surely had to outweigh those three tiny ants by a thousand to one, if not more. I nudged the feather. Still, they refused to let go of it. I had to respect their stubbornness. They were down right courageous as they looked up into the face of a twenty-two ton cat-creature looming over them, a creature who could promptly ponder the possibility of placing a *purrfectly* placed paw upon their heads, pulverizing them. Needless to say, these three ants minded their *p's* and *queues*.

I decided to help them. I would have to be very careful. I told them to brace themselves. On the count of three, using my right front paw (for it had to be the right one), I carefully eased the feather up and over them. I feared their legs might buckle. Then the feather began to move again. It seemed to move even faster now. I wonder if they were worried they'd be late for night school and wouldn't get a chance to do *show and tell* with their feather. I wished them good luck, but didn't dare tell them to *break a leg*! Any way you look at it, moving that heavy object had to be a *feather in their cap*!

I reconnoitered late into the night, having concluded that I would be spending the rest of the night outdoors anyway. Soon, the moon would be going down and, soon enough after, the sun, an even brighter orange ball, would be rising in the east, heralding the dawn. The lights had been turned out in the house hours ago and the feather had long since been transported to its destination. I decided to sleep in the old henhouse building. No longer used for chickens, the only thing in the old henhouse nowadays were garden tools and bales of straw. I knew I could get in through a hole that had been made by the woodchucks or some other hungry animal. I crawled through the opening. Inside, I knew immediately I wasn't alone. The black, beady eyes of a raccoon peered out at me from a far corner.

He grunted. He sounded like a pig, but I knew he was just welcoming me as a fellow creature of the night. Without any confrontation at all, we each settled down to sleep. As I slipped into slumber, I wondered why Ma had not given me a third come-in call.

The sun shone through the old henhouse window. Its warm touch on my face awakened me. I heard some Canada geese honking overhead as they made their way south for the winter. I was hungry. Mr. Raccoon was still sound asleep. I did my morning stretches, then slowly moved out of the building, being very careful not to wake him. The sunlight outside was blinding. I headed for the back cellar door. I knew Ma soon would be coming out it on her way to feed the barn cats. Sure enough, there she was! Something was wrong, though. She seemed depressed and was dragging her feet. I raced up to her. Immediately, her face brightened and she seemed very relieved to see me. She scooped me up. I thought she would squeeze me to extinction. She carried me back into the house and set me down before a feast the likes of which I cannot describe without beginning to dribble and drool.

By then, the barn cats had congregated at the back door. Ma was late for them, now. She looked out and laughed. She quickly gathered up the food and walked, very spryly I thought, out to the barn. She soon returned. She began to explain why I had been left out all night and why she was so relieved to see me. "I thought you were *dead*," she exclaimed, as she pointed in the direction of my quarters.

That morning she had expected to find me in my usual quarters. I was not waiting for her at the top or bottom of the stair steps, so she was sure I was still sleeping. But, when she found that I was not anywhere in sight, she began to think that I had eaten something bad, or some other malady had done me in. She checked under the old TV, under the furnace, and under the freezer. When she pushed her old broom under the laundry tub closest to the wall, she felt something slightly stiff, but kind of mushy soft. She thought sure it was me. No matter how much she gently prodded, I didn't move. As tears came to her eyes, she decided to feed the barn cats first, then she would come back to pull me out and bury me.

Then she saw me as she walked toward the barn. It dawned on her that I had been left out all night. Whatever it was back under the laundry tub, it wasn't me. She started to apologize for not ever making that third call for me, as was her habit. But, I stopped her. I should have come in on her second call, as I usually did. I should not have caused her any grief at all. Beside, I wanted to see what she thought was me under that laundry tub. Ma put a cardboard on the floor and knelt down so she could get back under the tub. She grabbed hold of something and slowly pulled it out. It was my mini-blanket! I had been rolling around in it and tossing it around. I forgot that I had left it under the tub. Was I embarrassed. Ma scolded me gently and said, "You know this really is going to the grave with you, but hopefully no time soon!" We both laughed and laughed. Later, I thought about poor Mr. Raccoon sleeping out in the old henhouse every night. I resolved to take him a mini-blanket as soon as I could.

Ice is into the nip! Ice is into the nip! ...
Now he's dreaming Santa's chewing bubble gum,
That every reindeer's chewing some.
And every time that Santa's bubble pops
His sky is filled with great big snowdrops!
And, when each reindeer's bubble pops,
His yard is filled with big red gumdrops!
Wow! Ice is zeeing zaws ... zeeing zip pop! pop! zip pop pop! ...

30

Christmas

A thick white blanket of snow had covered the ground last night. Everything looked so calm and peaceful. All the earth seemed to have snuggled up close together under this glistening white cover. It was the day before Christmas, and the snow had fallen just in time!

Snow can be so quiet. I never heard it coming down. It was cozy and warm in my apartment. I really had no desire to go outside. But Ma urged me to get some exercise in the snow. She had an ulterior motive, but I didn't know it then. Before long, we were engaged in a snowball fight. Ma was careful not to pack the snow too tightly. By the time her *snowballs* reached me they were nothing more than snow showers. But it was really pretty clever of her. Using this tactic, she rarely missed me. In turn, I would race by her, kicking up the snow so it would get into the open tops of her oversized boots. I was pretty clever, too.

After we got back indoors, Ma said she wanted to finish up my Christmas costume and let me try it on. If it fit, she wanted to get a nice photo of me in it. She had decided to wrap it up today, so to speak, so she wouldn't have to worry about it tomorrow. So I relaxed, while Ma worked to finish the costume. Then she and Pa started to wrap presents. I couldn't see what was being wrapped, so I couldn't relax anymore. I kept wondering what present Ma and Pa had wrapped for me. But, cats will be cats. Eventually, I drifted downstairs to my quarters for a mid-morning nap and soon fell fast asleep.

There was an unusual amount of activity going on upstairs. The commotion woke me up and brought me to the door to listen closely. I suspected Ma and Pa were hauling packages out of the closet. They always hid things in there until it was time to wrap them for Christmas. Suddenly...Thud! Then all was silent. What happened? I started to scratch at the door and began to meow loudly. Was everything all right? Could I sneak a peek at my present?

Ma opened the sliding door to see what I wanted. Good! She was OK, and I could hear Pa moving around in the adjoining room. As Ma reached down to greet me with a stroke to my head, a large spool of red ribbon, slipped from her grasp. It bounced all the way down the steps, unrolling a streak of red as it went. Of course, I was intrigued. I raced down the steps after it. I caught it as it made its last bounce at the bottom step. But, I couldn't stop and went zooming on by with the spool and all in my mouth. Ma had started down the steps and had stepped on a section of the red ribbon. Suddenly, I reached the end of the spool, so to speak. The ribbon went taut, held in place by Ma's foot, and the spool jerked back, sending me into the kind of sprawl that Hollywood would have appreciated in one of those old "B" movies. As I sprawled head over paws, Ma's foot released the ribbon as she proceeded down the steps. The spool then sprung forward again, along with all the red ribbon. By the time I stopped rolling you couldn't tell which red end of me was my head and which red end was my tail. I had managed to wrap myself up tighter than a mouse in a jar full of peanut butter. Ma couldn't stop laughing. The color of my face must have blended in nicely with the color of the ribbon.

Ma slowly, too slowly it seemed to me, unrolled me. She said I could keep the empty spool, and she'd use the ribbon to decorate the evergreen tree outside the house. Eventually, actually not long after the red had faded from my face, the empty spool became one of my favorite toys. And, Ma would often make it even more popular with me by tucking a bit of catnip into the hollow center space.

That afternoon arrived more quickly than I could have imagined it would. Ma came down the steps carrying my new Christmas outfit. There was a red stocking cap, a red romper suit, both trimmed in a white fluffy material, as white as the snow, and a poinsettia pennant, all to help me herald in the Christmas season. I thought of my practice session with the red ribbon as Ma carefully dressed me. Then we went outside for pictures.

Ma suggested I pick a good comfortable spot near the gaily decorated Christmas tree. I looked over at the evergreen. There was that red ribbon. Looking around I spotted a large bank of snow. It looked like a giant marshmallow. I thought it would make a perfect spot for me to pose gracefully, while Ma snapped a photo or two. I climbed atop its snowy crest. I meowed for Ma to take my picture and get this all, all over with. I watched her trying to focus the camera, as she moved closer and closer to me. Suddenly, I felt a sag beneath my body. Before I realized what was happening, I sank down into the marshmallow snow mound. Just at this moment, before I could stop her, she snapped my picture. Oh, *wow*. What would Hollywood ever think of me now? I probably could not have planned a better pose for a ridiculous and embarrassing grin! Still, I had managed to keep my grip on my poinsettia pennant.

Ma laughed. If you ask me, I think she had a few too many laughs that day. As I struggled to get up out of that snow bank, she promised to take another picture, if I'd let *her* pick the spot. No way, no dice, no sireee, bah humbug and forget Christmas all together!! There'd be no more pictures in red costumes for me. Ma didn't insist on another photo. So, all wasn't quite lost; I had to get back into the house and get out of my nice red wet costume, for after all, tomorrow was Christmas, and Ma didn't want a sick cat on her hands. Or, a really mad one.

All in all, I slept pretty good. You might say I missed the sound of Santa and his hearty *Ho! Ho! Ho!* But, here it was. Christmas day! What had jolly old St. Nick brought for me? Ma came downstairs early. She brought me a special breakfast, but I was only interested in what was beneath the Christmas tree. So, I let the breakfast sit untouched as I waited anxiously at the kitchen door. Soon, Ma opened the door and let me into the upstairs. I entered in a very calm, very sophisticated way. I *zoomed* in, in two leaps and a bound, landing right in front of the Christmas tree. There was more than one package with my name on it! I decided to ignore one of the packages, for I could smell what it contained. If I had gotten into the catnip, I'd surely have made a real mess of my other packages. There was a couple of pretty packages from Ma and Pa, a crazy wrapped package from Aunt Vivian, and one from my good friend Marian. There was also a neat package from my barn friends. I need not tell you about all the nice gifts I got, but one of them was the long-awaited privacy screen for my metropolitan bathroom!

I must have then turned to the package I'd set aside. This must have been what had made the loud *thud* I had heard the day before. It was filled with Cosmic Catnip. My favorite blend! I dipped my paw in and savored a quantity. I dipped my paw in again, and again. I was immediately transported to seventh heaven, or some equivalent galactic paradise! All I can remember is laughing and laughing and laughing, as I shouted to everybody, "Marwee, Marweeee Quismassss!"

The damaging sorrow
Of being lost in a dark surround
Is lost in the healing joy of being found.
For on the morrow,
Ever are we restored by the One light above
To someone we trust, to someone we love.

31

The Orange Stranger

Monday, January 5th. I remember the day well. We were having a severe cold spell. The sun was shining brightly that morning and the snow glistened in the sunlight. It cast an indescribable pristine beauty all about.

I could feel the cold penetrate through the glass of the north door window as I sat on my ledge and squinted out the window. Ma had done the laundry yesterday and the door window was completely frosted over, except for a small peep hole.

The snow lay deep on the ground. It must have snowed all night. Would I go to the barn this morning with Ma? Could I get there through all the deep snow? I decided to chance it, that is, if I could persuade Ma to let me accompany her.

She cautioned me that the snow was very deep and I would be challenged. But, I was determined to go. Finally, she relented. "OK, I'll make a good path for you to follow," she said as she pulled on her boots. I swear, she could not have survived the rigors of the country without those big boots of hers! Once out the door, Ma did not tarry, for the wind was biting cold. As soon as the wind hit my nose, I thought "Perhaps I should stay in after all." But, not one to be considered a sissycat, I flexed my deltoids and forged ahead. Already far ahead of me, Ma turned around and called encouragingly to me, "Come on Blackie. You can do it!" Sometimes I wished she would call me "Ice." This was sure the day for that name!

I made jackrabbit jumps from one of her footsteps to the next, as I brushed and dislodged piles of snow into each footprint. There was no way could I make things easy on myself. And, I tell you, it was cold! I could feel the vapors from my breath forming frost on my whiskers. I hoped my whiskers wouldn't freeze and break off! So, when I say I *hurried* from footprint to footprint, you know I wasn't moving too slow!

I was exhausted when I finally reached the barn. My paws, and especially my belly, were nearly frozen. It was a real relief to get inside the barn. As soon as I was inside, I made sure all my whiskers were still intact. They were, I'm glad to say. I shook off the snow that had caked on my fur coat as Ma congratulated me, "I knew you could do it! Told you it would be a challenge, didn't I?"

I greeted Bo and Fluff. They both looked quite well in spite of the cold. We exchanged news while Ma finished preparing their repast. It was very quiet in the barn, except for the crunching sounds made by Bo, Fluff, Shadow, Delsey and all the other cats as they eagerly ate their breakfasts. Just as Ma and I bolstered ourselves for the return trek to the house, we heard a timid, almost plaintive, *Meow, meowww.*

Ma called out, "Here kitty, here kitty!" A handsome, Ma would say *lovely*, orange cat emerged from the north stable. Where had he come from? Ma could not recall seeing it in the area. Was he another drop-off? He appeared to be in excellent condition. He appeared very healthy and not at all mistreated. He wasn't thin, or bedraggled, like Newcat was when he had arrived at the Berg Barn.

It didn't take much coaxing for him to come out and share some of the barn cats' food. They didn't object at all, as though they had already made their acquaintance with him. But Flow and Buff had not said anything to me about his presence, so I'm sure he had just then let his presence be known to us all. We decided to wait until he finished eating. We wanted to see how the other cats would react to him. They accepted him without any fuss, so we knew we could leave him in their custody.

The excitement of seeing the newcomer warmed me up; it did not seem nearly as cold outside as we headed for the house. This time, I led the way and Ma followed me. I happily jumped along, relieved that she had not brought the orange stranger back to the house with her. Half-way to the house, I looked back, still in a jovial mood, and shouted with a hint of sarcasm, "Come on, Ma. *You* can do it!"

All that day I thought about the stranger. Was he just passing through the area, through our neighborhood, so to speak? Was he lost? Would he stay?

Several months passed. The orange stranger had settled in to life in the barn amidst new friends. Bo and Fluff both agreed he was quite a gentleman and he got along well with everyone. It was very evident that he soon realized the Berg Barn served up the best *Bed & Breakfast* in these parts!

It was early March. Winter had relaxed her grip considerably. Ma and I noticed that *Stranger* had not eaten anything for three days. He was sneezing a lot, too. These things concerned both Ma and me. She was worried that he might have an upper respiratory infection, a viral sickness she had experienced with some of the barn residents over the years. It usually necessitated a trip to the Vet. Ma decided to have Stranger checked over. She called the Vet and got an appointment for Stranger that same day.

Ma gathered him up in her arms. He did not resist. In fact, he seemed quite content and willing to accept whatever Ma had in store for him. He was sick! Ma hurriedly prepared the cage, positioning it again on the corner of the ping-pong table, as she always did with each of us patients. Stranger would need it to recuperate in.

As Ma made preparations to leave, Stranger explored the new surroundings. He seemed less than enthusiastic, however. Mostly, he just sat and we looked, maybe kind of stared, at each other. I remember how thrilled I had been when I was brought into this big white house. He just sat there. Of course, I wasn't sick! He seemed a nice enough fellow. I thought we could get along nicely together here in the white house. After all, he had made friends with Bo and Fluff and all the other barn cats during his almost two-months stay with them. Soon, Ma turned her attention to placing Stranger in the cat-carrier.

Well, given my own past experiences at the Vet, I figured I wouldn't be seeing Stranger for a few hours at least. I decided to finish my breakfast and then take a nap. I figured I'd be well-rested by the time they returned. But, before I had time to drop off into a slumber, they were back! Ma placed Stranger into the cage. He still didn't look too good. I immediately jumped on the ping-pong table to welcome him home. My gesture of kindness fizzled. Ma had, as usual, covered the top and two open sides with black plastic. My view was thus restricted and it was not possible to even talk to him from on top of the table.

I did get to see Stranger twice a day when Ma gave him his medicine. He had to take a dropper full of two kinds of medicine every twelve hours! So I saw him when

Ma took him out of the cage to administer the dosages. Soon, he was feeling much better. Ma let him out of the cage and he was given freedom to roam, in my quarters! His appetite soon returned. In fact he had such a good appetite that I had to keep a close watch on my own food dish. He would clean it out if I had given him the chance.

With each passing day, he became more frisky and we began to have great fun together, especially when Ma played with us, too. We were especially fond of chasing after the long plume of ornamental grass she would wave tantalizingly close to us and then pull it back as we both lunged for it. It became apparent that we were going to become best pals in spite of my envy in having to share Ma's affections with him. I could see Ma was getting really fond of him, and Aunt Vivian praised his *loving disposition*.

One day, I heard Ma and Pa discussing Stranger. I listened through a crack in the kitchen door. "He must have been somebody's pet. He's been *very* well taken care of. He's even been neutered," Ma said. Pa agreed and suggested that Ma put an ad in the paper to see if someone would claim him. They decided to run an advertisement under LOST & FOUND reading:

Found: Large orange,
neutered male cat.
Loving disposition.
To claim or own,
Call 965-12345

I think we all wished, in our own way and for our own reasons, that there would be no response to that ad. But, there was! On the very evening the ad appeared, Ma received a phone call. It was a lady who lived about eight miles away. She told Ma she had lost her *Butterscotch* back in October of last year! She explained she had searched and searched for him. She had even offered a substantial reward for his return, all without success. She had all but given up hope. Ma and the lady exchanged details of Stranger as to identifying marks, colorations, mannerisms, and the like. The lady grew more and more excited. She and Ma agreed that, quite possibly, he was her Butterscotch. The lady said she would stop by in the morning to see him.

I saw a tear in Ma's eye. I know that she was excited to think that she might be playing a part in re-uniting a beloved pet with its owner. But, there could be sadness, too. I said nothing to Stranger, for I did not want to get him all pumped up, only to have it turn out that this lady was not his Ma.

Morning came. No way would I go wondering around outside this morning! I sensed the excitement of a possible dramatic reunion. Just then, I heard a car drive in and a second later Ma greeted someone at the door. No time was lost. They were coming down the steps, with Ma leading the way. I nudged Stranger forward, but I kept myself safely in the background, for I was taking no chances of suddenly being adopted. Of course, I knew deep in my heart, Ma would never sell or give me away.

The lady seemed very jolly. As soon as she saw Stranger, she picked him up, saying, "Are you my Butterscotch? Are you my Butterscotch? *You are my Butterscotch*!!" She was overjoyed. Although it had been six months since he had disappeared, he had not forgotten her. He quickly snuggled up to her neck. The lady had tears in her eyes. She exclaimed, "That's exactly the way he always snuggled up to me!" Just that quickly, they both knew they had found each other again; she, her Butterscotch and he, his Ma! My Ma had tears in her eyes, too. I have to admit, I was moved, also. It seemed that a miracle had taken place right before my eyes!

I knew that Ma would miss Butterscotch. I would miss him, too. On the other paw, I no longer had to share Ma's affections. And, my leftovers would still be left in my dish when I got hungry and decided to finish them up. Thus, the *epoch* of long-lost Butterscotch came to a very happy ending for all, I think.

I should add some thoughts, as an epilogue to this story: I truly missed him, but there were compensations to make up for his absence: For instance, I had my domain back all to myself; the back door ledge is no longer already occupied when I go to use it. And, it is quiet. Butterscotch seemed to mew a lot. Maybe he was thinking of his own home when he mewed, for he seemed at times to be almost crying out loud. And, I remember him jumping up on the ping-pong table to watch Ma nearby as she sat hooking a rug. He seemed fascinated by the click-click of the latch hook as it pulled and knotted the yarn into the canvas. Maybe it reminded him of his own Ma. But then again, whenever a piece of yarn accidentally fell to the floor, he was always quick to jump down from the table, cuff and toss the elusive piece into the air.

A few months before Butterscotch left, Aunt Vivian had brought me a wicker basket for a bed. For some reason I can't explain, I never used it. But, Butterscotch was quick to realize its potential and found it most comfortable. After he left, I decided to try it out, in order to find out what he liked so much about it. I then discovered how luxurious a wicker basket can be! I now have some wonderful dreams while sleeping there! Where my mind was before, I do not know!

I also admired Butterscotch for his fearlessness. He even dared to go where I would not, or more accurately, where I could not. His physique allowed him to access the dirt cellar. He could squeeze through a very narrow passageway between two stone walls. After he left, I tried many times to go through that chink in the wall, but I never could fit. I often wonder what he found there. I do know he found lots of cobwebs, for he would always emerge covered with them. All in all, I will never forget Butterscotch. I hope he is as happy as I am!

Our feline friends would never hassle us,
Would never give a tethered darn
Wether we sheltered them in a castle plus
Or shared an olde and weathered barn.

32

My Loyal Barn Friends

*T*here are, as they say, five million stories in the big city. Well, as you can see, there are a lot of stories here on the farm, too. So far, you've just heard some of my stories. All of my friends in the Berg Barn have lots of stories to tell, too. As a matter of fact, without their understanding and help, I would not have had it so good in the Berg white house. In fact, it was their willingness to join in, and to take a very courageous stand that made it possible for me to make my *Dream Come True*. They truly are my heroes, my friends, and my family. So, with heartfelt gratitude to them, I will try my best to describe each and every one:

Graydash - female. Light gray. Little on the heavy side, as tends to eat too much and doesn't get enough exercise. Shy, afraid of boy cats. Follows close to Ma's feet, knowing she will be safe there for the moment; then runs to her hiding place when Ma leaves the yard.

Creampuff - male. Cream color. Minds his own business, except for chasing girl cats. Seems to be growing more friendly. Calls me "Icey-nicey."

Midnight - male. Black. Very affectionate. Has a swaggering walk, perhaps caused by an early injury. Was a drop-off at the farm, before I came. A true comrade, for he made me feel real welcome when I first was brought to the barn by Ma and Diana.

Rusty - male. Dark orange. Came to us from a neighbor. Visited frequently, then decided to stay. Dominates the girl cats and even a couple of the males. Seems he would like to be friendly, but is very cautious.

Chelsea - female. Orange and white. Stays to herself a lot. Not much personality. Sits on barn sill, facing the house, watches and waits for Ma to bring out the food.

Nuisance - female. Black and brown, mottled. Very, very affectionate. Loving disposition. Always shows up when Ma is out in the yard. Frolicsome. Follows so close to Ma's feet that Ma has to be very careful not to trip over her. Is not really a real nuisance.

159

Mischief - female. Mostly black with splashes of brown. Good hunter. Does not always show up at mealtime. Affectionate and likes to be petted when around.

Whitey - female. White with a few splashes of rust. Likes to go hunting. Can be easily spotted out in the field. Sits, like Chelsea, and watches for food to be brought.

Bo - male. Tiger. Bo is my dear blood brother. Likes to show off, a fair hunter. Affectionate. Always around at mealtime.

Whispher - female. Tiger. Like Fluff, is delicate and demure. Nice disposition. Likes melon, too. Always around at mealtime.

Sootie - male. Black. Very affectionate. Likes to tag Ma to garden. Intelligent. Will lay down in Ma's shadow to cool off. Likes *cat*-a-tonic dog poetry.

Fluff - female. Cream color. My dear blood sister. Thick long hair. Demure, sweet disposition. Bo and I inherited all the rambunctious tendencies and left not an iota for her.

161

Sweetie - female. Mottled black/brown. Long hair. Sweet disposition. Likes tummy rubbed. I call her "Q.T." An eyecatcher. Aloof toward all the boys.

Delsey - female. Tiger. Very aloof personality. Mildly affectionate, tolerates some petting. Intelligent, likes to discuss philosophy.

Newcat - male. Black. Newest member of family. Has gained back his health. Affectionate and courageous. Likes to tell jokes.

Postscript

In conclusion, or *pawsing* to reflect on my *adventures*, let me make it *purr-fectly* clear, I have experienced so many events in my life to date, some good and some bad. Some good and some bad adventures, sure; but they have balanced out, and balance, I guess, is everything. (This is easy for a cat to say.) All in all, I have been most fortunate in having had the opportunity to be lifted from an empty parking lot into a loving family, where I was able to develop to my fullest potential.

I am proud that I have gone a long way toward developing a *live-and-let-live* philosophy. If I have learned anything, it is that all creatures great and small occupy an important place in our world, and all deserve our respect and as much love as we can give.

Ma has told me that I have been a joy to her. She says that I am the *Lamborghini* of the cat world in her eyes. She hopes that, if she ever has to give me up, my new parents will appreciate me, regardless of some of the annoying and sometimes unforgivable things I can do.

Lastly, I'm very proud to report that I've been voted *"Character Cat of the Year!"* By whom, you ask? Why, by Ma, of course!

Notes of Appreciation

A very, very special thank you to Dr.s Leonard and Jane Battig of *Cedarside Animal Hospital* for taking such good care of me, and so many of my feline barn friends.

***

Also, to C.H.E. Shire for the verses included in this work. "Smiley," as he is affectionately known to all of us, volunteered to visit the Berg Farm frequently from his horse-farm home a *fur* piece down the road from us in order to write the verses in this book. Our publisher asked me to add, as the editor put it, "an indi-*cat*-ion of uni-*verse*-al edu-*cat*-ion." One or two of the verses also came from Smiley's good buddy and fellow poet, A.C.A. Taca, whom we all know as "Ace." Though I think some of the cat verses of T.S. Eliot are very clever and amusing, to me poetry has always been somewhat mystifying, so I am indeed grateful for Smiley's contribution and Ace's help. Strange, when you look closely, how a name seems to fit some people so nicely. Smiley seems to be a very typical Cheshire, and Ace, when I would run into him at the farm, always seemed to be confused as to whether he was just coming or going.

...."Ice" Berg

The Sensitive "Traveler"

Other illustrated fine hardcover books published by PLANT*Speak Publications:

The TRAVELING BASKET, or Mrs. Carey's Christmas Call by Kathi Belford w/verse by K.A.Best...........
ISBN 0-9646803-6-X 19.95 USA

The TRAVELING BASKET II, Behn's Gift, and The Missing Hour Stories by Sally J. Wiseman and Kelly Boyer Sagert w/verse by K.A.Best......................................
ISBN 0-9646803-7-8 21.95 USA

The Purple Turtles Mystery, and The Legend of Lost Son by Kathi Belford, Jack Dean Smith, Editor ....
ISBN 0-9646803-2-7 17.95 USA

>Bout Boomerangs, America's Silent Sport by Kelly Boyer Sagert   Full Color, Art, History, Heroes..................
ISBN 0-9646803-3-5 29.95 USA

Please ask for these books at your favorite bookstore or local library.

xvi

Your Friend

My Favorite Photo

Hi, my name is _____.

I was born on _____.

I live in _____ with
_____and _____.

My favorite food is _____.
My favorite activity is:

_____
_____
_____